ANYONE
FOR
DIAMONDS?

ANYONE FOR DIAMONDS?

*Memoirs of an American Oil Man
in the Amazon Basin*

Donovan B. Grable

Reflections Press
Madera, California

Reflections Press
17 Seasons Court
Madera, California 93637

Published 1988. First Edition
Printed in the United States of America

Library of Congress Cataloging-in-Publication Data

Grable, Donovan B., 1905–
  Anyone for diamonds?

  1. Oil well drilling—Peru—Agua Caliente.
2. Salvage—Brazil—Manaus. 3. Grable, Donovan B.,
1905–   . 4. Petroleum workers—United States—Biography.
I. Title.
TN873.P52A383 1988   622'.3382'098   88-31751
ISBN 0-944709-05-2

DEDICATION

With fond memory to the adventurous men from the world over who helped open up the great Amazon Basin of South America—for better or worse. And, especially to the men of the oil and mining industries. And, to Evelyn Jo, who wanted me to do this long ago.

CONTENTS

Preface

The story *Anyone for Diamonds?* is based on several true experiences and episodes I encountered in South America from late 1938 through early 1939. It is an ongoing tale I have told, verbally and in fragments, many times in the past fifty years, to friends and companions. Recently, I have narrated it to my daughter Linda Grable-Curtis, who has assisted me in getting it all in writing. I have been encouraged by many people to write my memoirs—to share with others the adventurous undertakings I have experienced, especially those in South America, which apparently have a "romantic and exciting" ring to them.

My first book, *The Egyptian and Inca Gold Traders,* details my earliest visit to Peru in 1920 when I was fifteen years old, while accompanying my father. This book describes my later years and continual visits to South America, working not only in Peru but also Ecuador, Colombia, Venezuela, Brazil, and Argentina at various times until 1942. I made a comfortable living, primarily in the oil industry, at a variety of jobs, as a laborer, field supervisor and in equipment sales. The fortunes I made are the accumulated treasures of lifelong memories and friendships rather than those of monetary value.

Donovan B. Grable

In 1950, J. E. Brantly, president of Drilling and Exploration Company, Inc. (Drilexco), published an article in the company magazine, *Cuttings* (see appendix). In it he traced the story of Drilexco's involvement with drilling the first wildcat oil well at the Ganso Azul Concession in Peru (the Blue Goose Concession) on the Agua Caliente Anticline in 1938. The well site was located about four hundred miles southwest of Iquitos, Peru, near the center of the Peruvian jungle, and was probably as isolated as a place could be. The anticline's measurements were approximately twenty miles northwest to southeast in length, and nearly eight miles in width. It had a closure and reversal of about three thousand feet. The well was drilled at an altitude of approximately six hundred feet above river level. It required real ingenuity to get there—either by auto, plane, or boat.

That first wildcat well drilled east of the Andes in the Amazon Basin was completed as a producing well. It was an outstanding geological and mechanical achievement. The discovery of oil there was possibly the greatest single accomplishment in the area since the Europeans had found wild rubber plants and had invented uses for it. Five additional wells were later drilled and completed for production at Agua Caliente, yielding a supply of oil for the people living around the headwaters of the Amazon River.

Brantly mentions me in his article several times and explains why I was sent to Brazil and Peru in 1937: first, to salvage sunken oil drilling equipment to be used at the Ganso Azul Concession; and second, to work as a driller and as the camp boss at Agua Caliente.

The sunken three-hundred-and-fifty tons of drilling equipment was on the river steamer SS *Miguel Bitar,* which had wrecked on the Amazon River about thirty miles up from Manaus, Brazil, on November 30, 1938, on its way to Iquitos, Peru. The boat had been taking on wood for fuel and was caught up in the current; a huge mahogany log went through her hull and she sank. Salvaging commenced in January 1938.

Brantly's article does not describe (because he did not know) the sequence of events that took place and the details of the means, the methods, and the problems I encountered in traveling from the west coast of Peru to Manaus, Brazil, on to Iquitos, Peru, and finally to Agua Caliente, Peru. That series of events is retold here.

This memoir is studded with diamonds!—my inextricable and uncanny involvements with *the diamond*: that beautiful, rare, and durable gemstone which has fascinated mankind around the world throughout history. *The diamond*: whose major producers are South Africa, South-West Africa (Namibia), Angola, Australia, Russia, India, and *Brazil*.

Now—for the journey!

CONTINENT OF SOUTH AMERICA

CARIBBEAN SEA

ATLANTIC OCEAN

GUYANA
SURINAME
FRENCH GUIANA

VENEZUELA

COLOMBIA

ECUADOR

Rio Amazonas

PERU

BRAZIL

BOLIVIA

PACIFIC OCEAN

CHILE

PARAGUAY

ARGENTINA

URUGUAY

ATLANTIC OCEAN

THE GREAT AMAZON RIVER BASIN
AND LOCATION OF GANSO AZUL
(AGUA CALIENTE)

ATLANTIC
OCEAN

GUYANA

SURINAME

FRENCH
GUIANA

Rio Amazonas

Manaus

(Solimoes)

Belém

BRAZIL

J. E. BRANTLY
PRESIDENT

October 30, 1937.

CONTINENTAL BLDG : DALLAS, TEXAS
25 BROADWAY : NEW YORK CITY

TO WHOM IT MAY CONCERN:

The Bearer, Mr. D. B. Grable, is an employee of Drilling and Exploration Company, Inc. of 621 South Hope Street, Los Angeles, California, U. S. A., and will be employed in the capacity of an oil field engineer in the District of Masisea, Province of Ucayali, Department of Loreto, Republic of Peru, near the Ucayali River in the Amazon Basin.

This Company will assume the obligation of all transportation expenses for Mr. D. B. Grable's return to the above stated address.

DRILLING and EXPLORATION COMPANY, INC.

By _R W Marshall_
Vice-President

Signature of D. B. Grable

DB Grable

STATE OF CALIFORNIA)
                     : SS
County of Los Angeles)

On this 30th day of October in the year 1937, before me ATALA M. CARTER

_____, a Notary Public in and for said County and State, residing therein, duly commissioned and sworn, personally appeared R. W. MARSHALL, known to me to be the Vice President of the corporation who executed the within instrument, on behalf of the corporation therein named, and acknowledged to me that such corporation executed the same.

IN WITNESS WHEREOF, I have hereunto set my hand and affixed my Official Seal, at my office in the County and State aforesaid the day and year in this certificate first above written.

Atala M. Carter
Notary Public
My Commission Expires May 28, 1938

Letter of introduction for D. B (Don) Grable, from R. W. Marshall, Vice-President of Drilexco.

1

The Journey from Lima to Manaus

Lima

IT WAS EARLY DECEMBER 1937, when I arrived at Callao, the port for Lima, Peru, on a Pan American Sikorsky "flying boat." It had taken two days of daylight flying from the Canal Zone. (I had taken a regular plane from Miami to the Canal Zone.) I was met by the newly-appointed Drilexco agent, an American newcomer to Peru—Mowatt Mitchell. He was a real gentleman, but not too familiar with the oil man's way of doing things.

After dinner at the old Mowry Hotel in Lima, we decided the best way to get a handle on things was to meet at Mitchell's office the following morning and have the company attorney join us to lay out a way to get to Manaus, Brazil, on the Amazon River. By keeping the cable lines hot, at day's end we learned from the British Insurance Company, insuring the three-hundred-and-fifty tons of sunken cargo on the SS *Miguel Bitar* river steamer, that there was some reliable scheduled air and ship transportation from Belém on the east coast of Brazil to Manaus, twelve hundred miles upriver on the Amazon. The trip from Manaus to the location of the boat would consist of erratic transportation service.

The British Insurance Company had an agent in Manaus who spoke Portuguese, but no English or Spanish. However, their agent in Belém did speak English and Portuguese. The Belém agent, on the following day, advised us that the Brazilian government had a flying boat for military use and carrying mail. At times, the boat was available for extreme emergencies. However, it could not be relied upon because the military would not fly in bad or heavy weather (fog, rain, etc.). In those days no one could forecast weather conditions in the Amazon Basin.

After the second day, we had learned that cable messages would go through from Lima to Belém to Manaus much faster if they were sent in Portuguese. So, we found a stenographer in one of the banks who helped us with the cable problems. Four days later, after spending many hundreds of dollars in cables, it became apparent that if I were to get to the sunken *Miguel Bitar* by means of scheduled transportation (air or boat), it would take three to four weeks with "good-luck" connections. That timing would have made it too late to start the salvage operations because I had learned from the insurance agent that the river near the sunken boat is at its lowest in the months of December and January, the best time for salvage work. After then, the river starts rising at the rate of five to six inches per day until it reaches forty to forty-five feet in height at Manaus. Therefore, if we expected to recover anything out of the wreck, we would have to move quickly or wait for another year.

I relayed the information to our Los Angeles office, which in turn advised the insurance agents and me that, if it were humanly possible, we should start salvage operations at any cost as soon as possible. After receiving the message, I had Mowatt and the attorney contact the Peruvian military base at San Ramon, located on the east side of the Andes, to alert them that I would be on my way after obtaining a car.

The rainy season had already started in the high Andes and San Ramon had advised us that the road from La Oroya (a small copper mining village situated between 12,000 and 14,500 feet above sea level) to San Ramon was partly closed. Also, they said that if I could convince the military command of the urgency of my getting to San Ramon, they might help me make it through.

Traffic between the two towns was, at most, four or five small trucks and buses a day. The traffic was allowed to go *up one day* and *down the next.* From the floor of the valley to the top of the mountain there were only a few places on the entire road where cars or trucks could pass each other. I was aware that during the rainy season, slides could remove whole sections of the road and that it would take crews with picks and shovels days to rebuild the road to a passable condition. However, realizing the urgency of making my way to the scene of the shipwreck, I decided to tackle going as far as I could by car from Lima to San Ramon (via La Oroya) using any other means necessary, such as by animal or on foot, should auto service become impossible. Also, I knew I could obtain a military plane to take me on to Iquitos, Peru, from San Ramon.

Mitchell thought I was crazy when I told him to get me one thousand dollars in small-denomination Peruvian bills plus another thousand in U.S. currency in tens and twenties. He said I would be robbed and killed if anyone had any idea I was carrying that amount of money with me. My answer to him was that if I could get over the mountain as far as San Ramon, I had no idea what would lay ahead before I reached my destination, and at the time no one else did either. I sure as hell did not want to run out of money when so much was riding on my reaching the shipwreck and meeting the insurance carrier to begin the salvage operations!

I obtained the money and also purchased a fair supply of canned goods, including Klim powdered milk, because native animal milk was undrinkable. I also bought a supply of *soroche* pills for use at high altitudes. The pills help keep the oxygen supply in the body from getting too low. I also arranged for a car to meet me at the hotel at 6:00 A.M. and I left for La Oroya, which happened to be as far as the driver would take his car.

La Oroya and San Ramon

Just before dark, I checked into a pension (hotel), located above La Oroya at the sixteen-thousand-feet-high Andean pass. I learned that several trucks and a bus were waiting there (at the top of the mountain pass) to go *down* to San Ramon—after the cars and trucks (which had been stuck on the road below for two days) made it *up* to the top. It was cold and windy and the spits of snow were enough to freeze on my clothes. The *soroche* pills hadn't helped very much and whiskey made me feel worse.

About noon the next day, some of the road crews came up on foot and reported that the cars and trucks should be on top before dark. It was a good thing I received the message, because I was feeling so lousy and was about ready to go back to Lima and try some other approach to the problem.

The sun came out the next morning and I got a seat up front with the driver on a bus heading for San Ramon. We were the third in the line going *down* the mountain. There was no door on my side, which was next to the hillside. I felt I could jump out if necessary. The Perené River appeared to be a little white thread when I looked straight down from the road.

We arrived at San Ramon at about 4:00 P.M. during a slight drizzle. I met the military commandante and a number of his pilots. They were all very congenial and hospitable young men. However, the pilots appeared to be too young to fly. I had brought a good supply of whiskey, but thinking there was a possibility we might fly the next day, I decided it would be better if I offered to buy beer at the local *tienda* (bar). About ten of them were my guests at the *tienda,* where we drank up all the "hot" beer on hand. We made it to bed around midnight.

It rained all night, but the sun came out the following morning and we loaded two of the military's six old Stinson biplanes. The planes had been given to the Peruvian government by the United States when it was decided that they were too small for the U.S. Mail Service's coast-to-coast run.

The routine the pilots had to follow was to circle the San Ramon Airport until they reached an altitude of eight thousand feet. They were to travel in pairs. If a pilot reached eight thousand feet, say one-half hour before the other, he would have to wait for the other by circling around. The plane I was on seemed to have the heaviest load and I didn't think we would ever have enough altitude to fly over the mountain! The motor was spurting oil all over the windshield, so I could see out only part of the time. About three-and-a-half hours after takeoff, we landed in Pucallpa, a small town on the Ucayali River.

Iquitos

In the meantime, San Ramon had advised Iquitos by radio that I was on my way. They asked for a pontoon plane to pick me up at Pucallpa, along with an air force officer, and take us to Iquitos. We were fortunate, as the Stinson pontoon plane was waiting for us when we landed in Pucallpa. We boarded and arrived at Iquitos just before dark. I was met by the owners of the import/export firm, Israel and Company, who had been advised by Drilexco's Lima agent to be on the lookout for me. They were to give me any help they could (especially political assistance) in obtaining military services such as the use of air force and radio communications, which, as it turned out, they had already taken care of before I arrived.

The hotel I checked into had no running water or inside toilet. But there was a shower under a fifty-gallon drum, which was filled with water by a servant when he didn't have anything else to do.

Israel and Company were aware of everything that moved along the Amazon River system between Iquitos, Peru, and Manaus, Brazil. They were quite excited about the placer gold strike a Japanese prospector had made near the Blue Goose Oil Concession (Ganso Azul) above the Agua Caliente Anticline on the Pachitea River. It was not far from where we planned to drill the first wildcat well in the great Amazon Basin. The strike appeared to be of sufficient magnitude to attract an influx of enthusiastically welcomed outsiders.

I spent the next day with Mr. Israel, himself, who was a Jew, born in Peru, with British citizenship. He was charming and a keen businessman. I let him know how urgent it was for me to reach the site of the *Miguel Bitar* and that I would pay a bonus to any of the private boat owner/traders who would take me to Manaus.

I learned there were quite a number of the one-to-two-hundred-ton, steam-powered trading boats plying the rivers between Belém and Manaus and Iquitos. They would load up with items such as beer, *pisco* (a kind of liquor), gun powder and ammunition, toilet articles, and various drugs. One of the best-selling drugs was *jarabes,* a medicine taken to arrest syphilis sores, common among the river people. *Jarabes* was a heavy syrup laced with mercury and bismuth and many of the river people swore by it as a cure for syphilis. Medical doctors claimed that the drug was more effective in arresting the disease if the afflicted user also had malaria! Somehow, malaria competed with syphilis for control of the body of an infected person rendering the drug more effective. A very strange relationship!

There was so much to learn about the native river people as I came to understand their incredibly diverse racial makeup. The natives consisted of various Indian groups living all along the shores of the Amazon River system. These people—while maintaining strong tribal identities—continually intermingled with other tribes and had earlier mixed with *caucheros*—the early-day rubber harvesters (from about the turn-of-century to the mid 1920s). The *caucheros* themselves were of mixed and varied European and Indian ancestry. There was a good-sized colony of African mixture around Belém, but going upriver, very little African descent was evident.

Additionally, there were small pockets of several Latin-type people who had *not* intermingled with the local Indians. Their names sounded more Spanish than Portuguese. Many of the Latin people claimed no allegiance to any of the four countries that bordered the river—Brazil, Peru, Ecuador, and Colombia. For whatever reasons, they would, from time to time, pack all their belongings in canoes and move to any new location where they could raise crops for survival. The traditional farming techniques often yielded an abundance of crops and were obviously passed down to the natives from their ancestors who had been long accustomed to farming this terrain.

The river trading boats were all short on horsepower and had to stop every seven to eight hours to take on wood for their boilers. They had plenty of whistle power, though, and would blow their whistles in time for the natives to reach the boat landings with trade items such as otter and seal skins, tiger and spotted cat skins, live parrots and monkeys, and *paiche* meat. (*Paiche* is a huge fish, something like a sturgeon. The flesh is a very good food which can be salted and dried. It will keep for quite some time without losing its nutritional value. It was a staple food on the upper Amazon at the time I was there.)

Israel said there was a trading boat located about three days up the river from Iquitos, owned by a Spaniard who owed him quite a bit of money—about five hundred dollars. In 1937, five hundred dollars was a lot of money in that part of the world. Israel thought that if we could proposition the Spaniard and make him an offer in lieu of his debt, that he might be interested in cutting his trading short and taking me to Manaus.

After a half-day's discussion, we decided it would be asking too much of the Peruvian Air Force to fly me to the river landing where the Spanish captain was tied up making repairs on his engine. However, it was known that the British consul had a nice, custom-built riverboat powered with a twenty-horsepower Johnson outboard motor. He used it partly for business and partly for pleasure. The consul and Israel were not close friends, but Israel agreed to introduce me to him. (There was no American consul in Iquitos at that time.)

We arrived at the British Consulate during the cocktail hour. We were invited into the consul's office/study overlooking the river. It was a pleasant view. The consul asked us to join him for a "real" drink: scotch and soda on *ice!* Within a half-hour we found ourselves discussing mutual friends and acquaintances we both knew in Venezuela. I had been there from 1925 to 1930 working for the British Controlled Oil Field, Ltd., during the early oil booms at Maracaibo and El

Mene. At the same time, the consul had been attached to the British Consul General Office. The reminiscing lasted through two bottles of Old Smuggler! There was no problem in using the consul's boat to take me to the *Elena* and its captain the next morning. It took us about four hours to get to the landing and about one-and-a-half hours for the return to Iquitos later in the day.

I delivered a note from Israel to Captain Espinosa. After he read it, I told him why I urgently needed to reach Manaus. I told him I was prepared to pay off his indebtedness to Israel and pay him five hundred dollars more if he would cut loose and travel day and night—stopping only for fuel—until we reached Manaus. He agreed to the terms and he started down the river toward Iquitos shortly after I left on the British consul's powerboat. The captain docked at Iquitos around dusk and started loading supplies and fuel.

In the meantime, I caught Israel at his dinner table. He assured me he didn't mind receiving money while he was eating. So I paid off Espinosa's debt. I then changed some Peruvian money for Brazilian, checked out of the hotel, went to the dock, and boarded the *Elena*. It was still loading fuel.

Riverboat to Manaus

My assigned stateroom was comfortable with the exception of the cane mattress that smelled of mildew. I solved that problem by hanging a large, heavy-duty hammock I had purchased at Israel's store and had also used at the Iquitos hotel. The stateroom bed became a storage bin. The date was December 22, meaning I would be on the riverboat for Christmas and wouldn't be able to cable my love to my beautiful young wife, Evelyn, who was staying with my sister in Tampa, Florida.

We left the dock close to midnight under a three-quarter moon, which aided the night navigation. The captain estimated it would take us six-and-a-half days to reach Manaus, if fog didn't get too thick during the early morning hours.

The food on board was pretty good and we had ice for our drinks. There were two other passengers on board. One was a German woman who had been married to a Peruvian logger who had recently lost his life in an accident. They had no children and she was returning to her homeland in Germany. The other was a female teacher going to Leticia, Peru (near the international border between Peru, Colombia, and Brazil) to begin a new teaching assignment. There was a crew of eight.

We made Leticia on the morning of the second day and the schoolteacher disembarked. We also took on fuel for four hours and cleared the military and customs there—all a long, boring procedure.

Traveling on the yellowish waters of the Amazon through the "Green Hell" of the deep Brazilian jungle on a slow riverboat was monotony: day after day of the same scenery—the lush, thick, giant foliage only occasionally broken by a few thatched huts of a primitive village, or maybe some tropical birds or animals near the river's edge. The environmentalists needn't have feared man's destroying the Amazon Basin for quite some time! About noontime on the fifth day out of Iquitos, we sighted the wreckage of the SS *Miguel Bitar.* We landed and I took pictures of her and made a cursory examination of the river and the current. We then left for Manaus.

Manaus is located on the Rio Negro (the black river) near the confluence of the Negro and the Amazon. The two rivers, in fact, flow side by side for miles without merging. Captain Espinosa could not go up the Rio Negro to Manaus because he had no landing rights on the Rio Negro. The city was about fifteen miles from the Solimões Junction, where the two rivers finally meet. (Solimões is what the Brazilians call the Amazon River.) Therefore, the captain landed at the junction and we went ashore. We located a car to take the German woman and myself on to Manaus.

The captain advised us to check in with the local authorities before going to a hotel. I paid him and said good-bye to a friend who had taught me a great deal about river life along the Amazon in just one week's time.

East side of Andes, nearing 16,000 feet at La Oroya, Peru, 1937.

Pontoon plane for flight from Pulcallpa to Iquitos, Peru; Commander Fernandez of the local military, the pilot, and crewman; 1937.

Nº 11207

Yquitos, (Perú) 16 de Diciembre de 1937

Señor Drilling & Exploration Cº

_____ Debe

a Israel & Cia. Ltda.

Imp. "EL ORIENTE"-Iquitos.

NOTA DE DEBITO

1	Maquina Escribir (MR GRABEE)	160	-
1	caj. 250 Hojas Papel	4	-
100	Sobres aereas 46 3/4	3	50
6	Hojas Papel carbon	-	90
2	Archivadores	6	-
		174	40

las reclamaciones serán atendidas en las 24 horas desde la entrega de las mercacias que figuran en esta-factura

Bills: Israel & Company, Iquitos, Peru.

Yquitos, (Perú) 20 de Dicbre de 1937

Señor Don Grable

Provisions Voyage Manaos.   Debe

a Israel & Cia. Ltda.

Imp. "EL ORIENTE" - Iquitos.

NOTA DE DEBITO

1	carton 2 doc Cerveza				12.—
3	latas Queso				5.10
6	" Frutas				9.—
1	" Galletas Soda				6.—
					32.10

Las reclamaciones serán atendidas en las 24 horas desde la entrega de las mercancías que figuran en esta factura

Manaos Brazil.
Dec.29,1937.

Drilling & Exploration Co.
62I South Hope St.
Los Angeles California.

Gentlrmen:

I left Iquitos on the Arias a 200 ton river boat on the afternoon of Dec?2I,on the 22 we met the Morey a sister ship, she had I06 jts.of our pipe on board 4&5''d.p.and some 7.5/8 casing she had the hydromatic in the foward hatch. She was scheduled to arrive in Iquitos on the 24th. This was some of the cargo the Bittar left in Para.

On the 27th.about I8 a.m. we arrived at the scene of the Bittar,I am enclosing some photos of her you can probably tell more about her position,condition,ect.from one of them than you can from a dozen of my kind of letters.At best a sad sight.

Before Van left for camp we recieved a radiogram from Para stating that the Teniente Portello would leave Para about the 6th,pick up the barges and take them on up the river,we have all been under the impression she would arrive in Iquitos around the Ist.of Jan.

On my arrival here on the afternoon of the 27th.I find the barges still tied up here.

I saw Mr.Monteiro yesterday morning at 8 o'clock he says that the Portello up here to replace the Bittar,but was orderd back to Para,he dident seem to know why she was orderd back.

Mr.Monteiro says they now plan on sending the Bello Horizonte up from Para within the nexy day or so to arrive about the tenth of Jan.then transfer the cargo from # I barge onto the Bello and take the other two in tow and go on to the location.Mr. Monteiro is Paes's agent here.

I saw Mr.Dryer about I0 a.m. yesterday he is the Royal!s agent here and he informed me that divers say that salvage of the Bittar's cargo is impossible until the river recedes in Aug. or Sept.and then with chances of only part recovery a lot depending on the amount of sand and silt the river deposits over her.

As soon as I got this information I wired Israel in Iquitos asking him to relay on to Agua Caliente, Lima,and Los Angeles.

This afternoon at 4 p.m.Mr.Dryer called to say that he had a cable from Para urging him to start salvage at once, so the rest of the day we put in looking for the diver.

No one I have seen so far seems to be at all perturbed over the existing conditions and I hope I havent overstepod my authority by trying to impress on the fact that the time element means a lot to us,since the high water on the Pachetea will be a gamble after Feb.

start at once to make out a list of what was on the Bittar. I have all of Vans papers here with me and will

Letter to Drilexco, Los Angeles, from Don Grable in Manaus,
Brazil.

Although these papers are not supposed to be accurate they will be
something to go by in case salvage does start in the near future.

If you have been in the dark on your end as much as we
have been on our end this will all be news to you,and if any thing
else shows up I will push it on up the line for relay.

I am sending Mr.mitchell a copy of this letter and asking
him to foward Van one,Van will recieve it much quicker via Lima
than he would if it beat its way up on one of these river boats.

Fri.3p.m.30th.

A late cable from Para recieved by Mr.Dryer instructs
him to proceed with salvage operations,the divers are on hand.

Saw Mr. Monteiro at noon he says he has the Bello is on
her way up.I wired Israel soon after with instructions to relay.

According to Mr.Dryer it will take several days to get
salvage equipmentready at the same time he plans to get the legal
routine in order and be ready to start work on Jan.I.

It seems no one knows just how the Bittar was loaded
besides Van,and if I remember right he told me the derrick was in
the foward hatch left hand bow side,and the II.3/4 foward right
hand bow side foward hatch with22D,000'of 2" and some 3" on top
of it,if you plan on me staying here with the salvage,a scetch
from Van on the way she was loaded might aid us in getting out
the things we need most and first.

My adress will be Hotel Grande Manaos Brazil until I
hear from you.

Sincerely Yours.

D.B.Grable

2

Manaus:

Rats and Diamonds

Arrival

THE DRIVER WE HIRED to take us in to Manaus knew the agent for Drilexco's insurance carrier, Mr. Dryer of the Royal Insurance Company, Ltd. The driver took the German lady and me to Dryer's home. The agent was a German national who spoke some English. We arranged for him to accompany us to the hotel as well as go with us to register with the military and customs officials the following morning.

We were late checking in to the Grande Hotel, owned by a Spaniard, Ramon Telles, and his brother, Juan. They had come to Brazil in the booming days before World War I and made a fortune trading in rubber. They put their money into Manaus real estate; but when the crash came, they were stuck with several buildings and could not raise enough money out of their holdings to leave the country. They decided to ride out the troubled economy at a place where they owned a little something. In 1937-38, Manaus had a population of about seventy-five hundred. (I received this information before going upstairs to bed.)

I wasn't surprised to see termite droppings on the table and dresser tops. I put up my mosquito net over the bed and turned in before 10:00 P.M., when all electric lights were turned off at the city generating plant.

Laying in bed, I was startled by noises like a big cat or dog racing around in the space between the rafters and the ceiling. The ceiling material was beaten *chonta* palm, which looks like beaten bamboo, but makes a stronger and better ceiling material than bamboo. I got out a flashlight and tried to see what kind of animal could make such noises. I remembered years ago staying a few nights in a house in the high Andean town of Huancabamba, Peru, where *cachules* (small opossums) made so much racket I had to move out. But, never had I heard such sounds as these: that of several animals of some kind racing from one end of the building to the other in the ceiling! Sometimes it sounded like one would fall and hit bottom and then bounce up and run on another level. I stayed under the mosquito net until about daylight and then arose and went downstairs, just as a few fruit vendors were beginning to hawk their wares. I decided to walk down to the river pier, and there I discovered who all of the night noise makers at the hotel had been.

Rats

There was a group of rat trappers who had several varieties and sizes of rat traps that contained the captured rodents. A city official would count a trapper's rats, then take his trap over to the water's edge and drown them. The official would then return the trap to its owner with a slip of paper indicating the number of rats he had delivered. The trapper would supposedly turn in the number for payment elsewhere.

Fish, some appearing to be two to three feet long, would make the water "boil" around the place where the dead rats were released. And, on the opposite side of the pier, men carrying two-to-five-gallon cans on a wooden shoulder bar were dumping raw sewage from the cans into the river. The fish would boil as each container was dumped.

I returned to the hotel as Don Ramon Telles was opening up. I told him about the terrible night I had spent without a wink of sleep. He said that that was the experience most foreigners have when they first arrive in Manaus, and that most get used to the rat noises in time. However, he said he could move me to a room on the ground floor that was warmer but not nearly as noisy as the second-floor room, and he would furnish an electric fan. We agreed to the change and went to breakfast together.

During breakfast, which consisted of pineapple, *café con leche* (coffee with milk), hard rolls, American Golden State canned butter, and British Cross and Blackwell jam, he gave me a thorough briefing on his life since he and his brother, Juan, had come from Barcelona, Spain. At the start of the boom days, in 1910, they opened a food supply store to handle fine wines and European foodstuffs with money that they borrowed from their father. At the end of two years they were able to pay back the borrowed money. He and his brother would take turns going back and forth to Spain, at least once a year, to purchase the best European merchandise money could buy at the time.

Now, by the time the first hard breakfast rolls were placed on the table—while Don Telles was giving his dissertation—I could see rats poking their heads out of several holes around the baseboard and walls of the dining room. No one paid any attention to them. As other patrons came in, rats would scurry across the room to the other side. No concern!

Telles continued, telling me he was a proud civic leader and a driving force behind the building of the ornate new opera house. (The opera house is currently a tourist attraction in Manaus featuring a stage for folkloric performances.) Built with "rubber baron" money, this opera house was designed to rival the great concert halls of Europe. Telles was also instrumental in paving many of the streets and had helped sell the idea of installing a sewage system under the streets of Manaus. He said the main reason it was almost impossible to eliminate the rat scourge was because the rats could easily travel from one side of the city to another without coming to the surface: they traveled via the open sewer pipes.

Shortly after the sewer mains had been installed, the Crash came and the newly-planned water system lines (paralleling the sewer lines in many cases) were never hooked up.

Salvage Arrangements

We were almost finished with breakfast when Dryer, the German insurance agent, came looking for me. With him was one of his staff, Mike Monerio. We all sat down in the dining room. Before we delved into the problems we were to work on, I inquired about the German woman I had traveled with from Iquitos. Dryer said she was staying with him and his family and they would see to it that she returned home safely.

The first thing we agreed on was to advise our respective offices that we had made contact with each other and were working out a plan for the salvage of the *Miguel Bitar*'s cargo. I had already decided that a great deal of the cargo could be retrieved if we could obtain divers and a crane ship with enough power to lift the heavy items. We also needed to remove the upper deck and part of the second deck where most of the cargo was stored. After some exchange of cables with Belém during the morning, we located a Lamport and Holt crane ship and four Greek divers with diving equipment. We arranged their departure and scheduled them to arrive at the shipwreck ten days later.

I then went with Dryer and Mike Monerio to Augusto Lima's Officina de Carpentaria Naval (boat builder) just on the edge of town. There we arranged for the hourly rental of the fastest boat on the Upper Amazon. The boat was to be for my sole use for as long as required. At the same time, Dryer ordered, through Augusto Lima, to have an *alvarenga* (a barge) to be taken to the wreck along with hand tools and supplies for twenty river men to start tearing out things that would be in the way of our salvage operations. The expected arrival for the barge would be in two day's time.

The Departamento Dos Carreios E Telegraphas (telegraph office) was a block away from the hotel. I encountered a probem on my first attempt to send a cable to the Los Angeles office caused by inaccurate translations between Spanish, Portuguese, and English. Expecting to be using the cable office on a daily basis, I first thought about asking Don Ramon for help translating from Spanish to Portuguese. Then I thought about asking Dryer or Straussberger—another German agent working with Dryer—to do the translations, but decided against that in case there were problems with the settlements of the damaged cargo. Dryer and others would know too much about something that might have legal ramifications later on.

I inquired of the office manager of the telegraph office if he knew of anyone qualified to do English to Portuguese translations. He replied that he would send me a teacher after school hours, whom I could interview for help. It was getting close to noon—hot and sticky—and about the time river people eat and take a two hour siesta. I was tired and was all for the Latin custom of the two hour afternoon nap, so I returned to the hotel.

My new room was a much better and quieter one. I fell asleep and didn't awaken until one of the houseboys rapped on my door saying someone wanted to see me in the lobby. There were six or eight people in the rather spacious lobby. One was a coal-black man at least six-feet-eight-inches tall, who couldn't have weighed over one-hundred-fifty pounds. He was dressed in snow-white clothes, carried a briefcase and umbrella and was smiling from ear to ear.

Guilherme Johnson introduced himself as a professor of literature and a teacher of English in the local high school. At first I had some difficulty understanding him because he spoke English with a Trinidad accent, which he called "the King's true English"! I made an agreement with him to be on call seven days a week to translate my cables into Portuguese and to take them to the telegraph office to be sent out as soon as possible. He was to keep his own time and his pay was to be about one dollar per hour in Brazilian money, which was very good pay in Manaus.

My pace had been so hectic that I didn't realize it was New Year's Eve; there was no fanfare or big celebration for either Christmas or New Year's in Peru or Brazil, although both are Catholic countries. (They celebrate Christmas on a different date.) I exercised my new translator for the first time with a cable sent out under my name to my wife asking her to write to me at the Grande Hotel in Manaus.

Don Ramon Telles

During any breaks in my time schedule, I would try to be with Don Ramon. He had a manner that made a person realize that here was a high-quality man, with a head full of good common sense. I estimate that he was then in his early fifties, about five-feet-nine-inches tall and well-built. He had very light skin and dark hair and eyes. He wore a small mustache which had a little gray in it. He was a sharp-looking and quick-acting man.

On one occasion I asked Don Ramon about his brother, Juan, who would never speak to anyone unless forced to and who would sit motionless for hours staring into space. He replied that his brother suffered a nervous breakdown when their newly accumulated wealth disappeared during the Crash and they couldn't make their annual trips to visit their father in Spain. As his depression grew worse, he would vent his anger at the British by making long speeches in Spanish condemning them for stealing the rubber plants from Brazil and replanting them in Indonesia, which eventually brought about the collapse of the rubber industry in Brazil.

Don Ramon continued: in the last three or four years, his brother had forgotten about the British and was now venting his anger on Americans in speeches in Spanish. But people in Manaus paid no attention to him at all. The brother wouldn't speak Portuguese unless forced to against his will. I told Ramon that I wanted to hear the rest of the story explaining why Juan's number one hate was Americans and no longer the British, but that it would have to wait until I returned, because I was then leaving for the first launch trip from Manaus to the *Miguel Bitar* with Dryer and Mike.

Launch to Miguel Bitar

We walked from the hotel for quite a distance, past the pier where the rat drowning and sewage dumping took place, to where the launch, *Theresa,* was moored. The smell there was worse than at the other pier because it was near a fish cleaning plant and a slaughter house. Without exaggeration, I can tell you there were thousands of buzzards fighting seagulls for the fish and animal carcasses. And, when any remains reached the water, all kinds and sizes of fish would stir up the water, making it boil. When we left the mooring, I told all hands that from now on we find another place for the *Theresa,* even if we have to take a car to get to it. Augusto Lima operated the boat with one helper on the first trip; he would do so again on some later trips. The journey took three hours upriver and one hour for the return to Manaus.

With Don Ramon's permission, I had the hotel chef order enough canned goods, bottled water, soft drinks and other non-perishable foods to feed ten people for three days. The foodstuffs were to be kept on board at all times during the salvage operations. There were to be *no alcoholic drinks* of any kind—period!

Upon arrival at the wreck site, we were met by the priest from a village across the river, who had come to bless the operation. Before the rain started I proceeded to list quite a number of small items which had been recovered so far. I listed the losses which would have to be replaced because they were not salvageable. These included: drill string, outboard motors, a truck, gasoline, oils, and miscellaneous canned foods. When the rains came, we left for our return to Manaus and arrived at the hotel about dark.

Diamonds

As always, a crowd of idle people had gathered around the hotel entrance to watch and listen to the foreigners talk. At times the crowds would be so large that the guests would have a problem entering the lobby. But when the street lights went out at 10:00 P.M. most of the crowd would disperse. The hotel did have a doorman who kept the crowds out of the lobby.

Anytime I went in or out of the lobby, I would be surrounded by beggars, pimps, and vendors selling straw hats and snake and alligator skin articles. I said *no* to everything, because if you ever bought anything, they would never leave you alone.

That night there was an old Indian who was very persistent in having me look at whatever he had in a small cloth package. Supposedly, it was worth about five hundred dollars in Brazilian money, or fifteen hundred dollars in American money. I thought it must be gold. A day or so later, when I went outside the hotel, he fell in walking behind me muttering something in a hushed voice. I asked him to return to the hotel with me so I could get someone to be a witness for whatever it was he was trying to sell me for so much money. Don Ramon was in his room, so I sent a houseboy to ask him to join us.

When Ramon came into the lobby, partly dressed, I told him the Indian man had been talking to me every time I went out of the hotel during the past few days, and had even started following me. I told him that the Indian insists I look at something he has in the cloth package that is worth a lot of money and which he would sell to me for five hundred dollars in Brazilian money. Ramon said he had seen the man around town for many years, but didn't know what it was he wanted to sell to me. He thought the man was a *mestizo* (half-breed Indian) from the Upper Rio Negro. Don Ramon also reminded me of the very rigid law and penalties involved in trafficking in any of the precious metals and stones. All precious metals and stones must be sold to the National Bank of Brazil.

Don Ramon asked the man what he had in the package. He replied that it was *diamonds*. He started to undo the package, which was tied with a piece of string when Ramon stopped him and told him to return the package to his pocket, which he did. Ramon then motioned for all of us to sit at a table in the dining room, and reminded the man of the serious trouble he could get us both into if I bought the diamonds from him and it was reported to the authorities.

The old man said he had no money to take the diamonds to Belém, the nearest authorized place to buy and sell diamonds. And, in fact, Belém had not been buying at all in the last two years. When they did buy, they cheated you out of most of them, he added.

The old man reached into his pocket and retrieved the small bundle and bounced it in his band saying there was enough value in it to take care of him until he died, if only he could sell them. He then opened the package and it contained quite a number of little white-looking pebbles. I asked the old man how he knew they were diamonds, because they looked just like quartz pebbles to me. He answered that where he got his diamonds there were no quartz pebbles.

Remembering a Diamond Experience

I told the Indian man (while Don Ramon translated from Spanish to Portuguese) that my only experience with diamonds had been a bad one. I then related how it was during the heart of the Depression—1932—in Long Beach, California. I was down to my last twenty dollars in a strange city trying to collect money on some bad debts at a pool hall where oil field workers checked in and out to learn where they could find work.

I was standing in front of the pool hall, while my partner had gone for our car, when I was approached by a well-dressed, husky young man. He asked if I was a stranger in town and I replied that I was. He said he was too and was really needing some money right away. He asked if I would give him twenty-five dollars for a three-carat diamond gold ring, which cost three-hundred-and-fifty dollars new and for which any pawn shop in town would lend one hundred dollars. I replied that I didn't have the twenty-five dollars, and besides, I wondered; if the pawn shops were willing to lend one hundred dollars on it, why hadn't he gone to a pawn broker and borrowed the money himself.

He answered that he had taken the ring off the hand of a card shark he had nearly beaten to death for cheating him out of his last week's paycheck, and if he appeared at any of the pawn shops with the ring, the law would be waiting for him. But no one would know me and how I got the ring. I told him he was wasting his time on me because I was in town trying to collect some money on bad debts myself. Then the guy started coming down on the price and pleaded for fifteen dollars and finally ten dollars. I reached in my pocket and took out one of the four five dollar bills I had and bought the ring from him.

A few minutes later, my partner showed up and I greeted him telling how this must be our lucky day. We hadn't collected any of the bad debts, but I had just made one hell of a deal! I had paid five dollars for a three carat diamond and gold ring that we could take to the pawn broker who would loan us one hundred dollars on it—enough to get us home! He looked at the ring and said it looked genuine to him, so we left for Pine Avenue where the pawn shops were located. We parked the car and went in to one of the larger ones.

A fat, squinty-eyed, dark-skinned, Mediterranean-type of man asked if he could help us. We asked if he lent money on diamond rings. He replied he lent more than anybody else in town on good stuff and asked what we had. I took out the ring and handed it to him. He took one look through his glass, scowled, and said—with belittling sarcasm—that it was costume jewelry that could be bought across the street at the Kress five-and-dime store for fifty cents apiece!

Don Ramon, who had been translating the story, until I reached the part about how the ring could be bought for fifty cents, broke out in laughter. He never finished the ending to the story so that it would make sense to the old Indian. At any rate, I thanked the old man and told him there was no way we could do business together. Ramon ushered him out of the hotel. However, that never deterred the old Indian from taking every chance he could to talk to me and ask for an offer on his diamonds. In fact, a couple of days later, late in the afternoon when I returned to the hotel, he greeted me again. He had come to tell me that he had to dive into deep water for his diamonds and that there were no other stones like them in the river.

More About Rats

Translating the story of my disastrous diamond-buying deal put Don Ramon in a relaxed mood after his laughing spell. So, I reminded him he was to finish telling me why his brother had switched from hating the British to hating the Americans. Well, it seems some of the more civic-minded citizens in town had decided to seek help in starting a rat control program. An American firm from New York City was employed and the firm sent down a man, at Manaus's expense, to study the situation.

Apparently, the company's representative was a heavy drinker and spent most of his time at alcoholic drinking establishments or sleeping off hangovers. In a report, he wrote that the only way Manaus could ever eradicate its rat problem would be to plug all the buried sewer lines and continuously use the rat poison his company would supply. When he departed, he told city officials he would send them free samples of the recommended poison. Several months later two drums of the poison arrived and were brought to the hotel for trial and storage. Manaus didn't have the money to plug the sewer lines and the poison didn't seem to work. Don Ramon reported he still had two fifty-gallon drums full of the rat poison and not one rat had been killed. Everyone had entertained such high hopes of getting rid of the rats, and their disappointment was the reason Don Ramon's brother hated Americans: he felt that Americans had taken advantage of them.

I told Ramon I couldn't believe a licensed New York exterminator would send rat poison that didn't work; especially since the company expected to do future business with Manaus. Since it was getting late—around dinner-time—and Ramon was busy, and I was scheduled to go to the *Miguel Bitar* early the next morning, we agreed to meet later the following day when I would try to obtain the name and address of the poison supplier and contact them by cable to ask why the poison was not working.

I met Don Ramon who took me into a dark, dank storeroom where there were all kinds of old suitcases, clothes, shoes, and boxes of miscellaneous items—all coated with mold and mildew and rat droppings. The two fifty-gallon drums were there; one with its top partly cut open. The substance in the open drum looked like Epsom salts. There was no scent or odor. On top of the other drum, written in bold letters, was "POISON, Handle With Care, Use Gloves."

There were instructions for the use of the rat poison, which read something like: "To be effective, place a thin layer of poison on a slice of bread and cover it with a coat of sugar. Place the bread and a pan of water near rat runs. When the rat eats the bait, it will want water badly. When it drinks water, it will die instantly." Then the name and address of the manufacturer were listed.

I translated what I read on the drum into Spanish and asked Don Ramon if they had followed the instructions. He answered: "Hell no! We just put it out on the floor in a dish and said 'come and get it' " or Spanish idioms to that effect.

I asked Ramon to get some bread and sugar and a pan of water, while I went to my room for my work gloves. We would test the procedure right there in the room where rats were squeaking and running around and over our feet. A few minutes later we put the bait down and closed the door to make it dark. We went to a dining room table and ordered a soft drink. When we finished our drinks we returned to the storeroom and opened the door. Around the water pan there were eight dead rats and many others running frantically around in circles!

Don Ramon was not the typically excitable Latin-type. However, he was visibly excited at the scene before him and said, "*Gracias a Dios estoymos salvado,*" which meant: thank the Lord, we have been saved. He then went out to give the word to some of the other participants who had helped finance the expense of bringing the exterminator to Manaus.

That same evening, there was a great deal of activity at the hotel. I donated a pair of my work gloves to the cause. They were needed to handle tools to break up the poison, which had solidified to some extent. By 10:00 P.M., over one-half of one drum of poison had been taken to other sections of town and put to use.

The next morning the trappers were having a field day, to say the least. Thousands of rats were scurrying in all directions trying to find water. They were dying in the streets wherever water was dripping from rooftops. The trappers had met with the rat buyer who had agreed to allow credit for all dead rats, even if they were bloated, but no credit was given for older, decayed, and dried rats.

Fish market and slaughterhouse at pier area on the Rio Negro, Manaus, Brazil, 1938.

The sunken riverboat, SS Miguel Bitar, on the Amazon River near Manaus, Brazil, 1938.

(Interpreter)

Guilherme Johnson
~~LECCIONA INGLEZ~~

Informa-se sobre as obras da casa
Editora W. M. JACKSON, Inc.,–Rio
Thesouro da Juventude, Encyclopedia
e Diccionario Internacional, Historia do
Brasil. Diccionario de Candido de Figuei-
redo, eto.
Troca e compra sellos uzados.

Rua Quintino Bocayuva, 201

THE AMAZ-N TELEGRAPH COMPANY, LIMITED.
(CABO SUB-FLUVIAL DO AMAZONAS)

N.º

N.º de expedição	Expedido á	TAXA	Carimbo da estação
	ás		
	por		

Estação de origem	N.º de palavras	Horas	Data	Observações

Nome e endereço do Destinatario

GRABLE
901 SOUTH ROME ST.
TAMPA. FLORIDA.
WRITE VIA LIMA.
LOVE DON.

Peço que' o Telegramma acima seja transmittido conforme as condições especificadas no outro lado desta forma.

Assignatura

Endereço

First cable sent from Manaus with help from interpreter Guilherme Johnson.

Charge to the account of _Rec. Jan 17-38_

1256

$ ___

WESTERN UNION
CABLEGRAM

R. B. WHITE
PRESIDENT

NEWCOMB CARLTON
CHAIRMAN OF THE BOARD

J. C. WILLEVER
FIRST VICE-PRESIDENT

CHECK

ACCT'G INFMN.

TIME FILED

Send the following message, subject to the terms on back hereof, which are hereby agreed to

JANUARY 6th, 1938.

COPY OF CABLE SENT TODAY BY ROYAL INSURANCE COMPANY, LTD., TO THEIR PARA AGENTS

ASSURERS REPRESENTATIVE MISTER BRABLE NOW AT SCENE OF DISASTER PLEASE GIVE
HIM FULLEST COOPERATION SUPPLYING HIM ALL LABOR MATERIAL AND OTHER HELP
HE MAY DESIRE ENABLE HIM RECONDITION CARGO IN ANY WAY HE DEEMS PROPER
REGARDLESS OF EXTRA EXPENSE ENTAILED.

Modelo 561 / Antigo T 11

DEPARTAMENTO DOS CORREIOS E TELEGRAPHOS
=== TELEGRAMMA ===

PREAMBULO	Especie _____	Numero _____		Data _____ Hora _____	
	Origem _____	Palavras _____		Via a seguir _____	
	(O preambulo é preenchido no Telegrapho, excepto via a seguir)				Carimbo da Estação

ENDEREÇO	Indicações de serviço taxadas			TRANSMISSÃO
	Destinatario _Melita Iquitos._			HORA:
	(Rua, Avenida, etc.)	(Bairro)		Iniciaes do Operador
	Cidade _____	Estado _____		

TEXTO E ASSIGNATURA

Insurance agents report start salvage Bittar cargo at once

stop. Bello on way up. stop Advise Los Angeles.

Don

Cable communications with the insurance carrier.

THE AMAZON TELEGRAPH COMPANY, LIMITED.
(CABO SUB-FLUVIAL DO AMAZONAS)

No. 484

REDE DA COMPANHIA

No. de recepção	Estação de origem	No. de palavras	Apresentado às	Data
12	LOSANGELESCALIF	46	23.00	12

| Observações | WU WTN | Recebido de SA às | 10.36 por | A |

Nome e endereço do Destinatario: LC GRABLE HOTEL GRANDE MANAOS

GANSO AZUL REQUESTS YOUR OPINION ON FOLLOWING
FIRST DO YOU BELIEVE IMMEDIATE SALVAGE PRACTICA-
BLE SECOND WHAT IS YOUR ESTIMATE TIME REQUIRED
THIRD WILL CONDITION OF PACHITEA PERMIT FORWAR-
DING CARGO IMMEDIATELY AFTER SALVAGE STOP
THIS INFORMATION NEEDED FOR ESTIMATES OF COSTS

Received 11 am Jan 12. DRILEXCO

Para ser attendida qualquer reclamação em respeito a este telegramma, é preciso ser acompanhada por esta forma.

THE AMAZON TELEGRAPH COMPANY, LIMITED.
(CABO SUB-FLUVIAL DO AMAZONAS)

No.

No. de expedição	Expedido á		TAXA	Carimbo da estação
	ás			
	por			

Estação de origem	N.º de palavras	Horas	Data	Observações
	32			

Nome e endereço do Destinatario: MLT Drilexco Losangelescal

Part salvage pratical dependent river thirty to fortyfive days
authorities pachetea claim shipping possible but variable upto
stop
april fifteenth not after ten weeks salvage transportation unallows
much time

Peço que o Telegramma acima seja transmittido conforme as condições especificadas no outro lado desta forma.

Assignatura

Endereço

Cable communications regarding feasibility of salvaging equipment from SS Miguel Bitar.

OFFICINA DE CARPINTARIA NAVAL

Construcção de Embarcações de madeira de qualquer especie, reparação em Embarcação de madeira.—Installações de motores de explosão, etc., etc.

Rua José Paranaguá N.º 711

Manáos, 20 de Janeiro de 1938

O Snr. *D. B. Grable* Deve

a AUGUSTO LIMA

De duas viagens em lancha a motor de Manáos ao local do naufragio do vapor "Miguel Bitar" 18 horas de navegação a 25$000 a hora Rs 450$000

Recebi Manáos 20 de Janeiro de 1938

Reis...450$000.

RECEBI do snr. D. B. Grablo, a importancia de Quatrocontos o cincoonta mil reis, 0450$0000 provonientos de descito horas de navegação em lancha a motor, do porto desta cidade ao local ondo-se encontra naufragado o navio "MIGUEL BITAR"!!

MANAUS, Janeiro de 1938

Bill from Augusto Lima, Manaus, Brazil, for use of motor launch to Miguel Bitar.

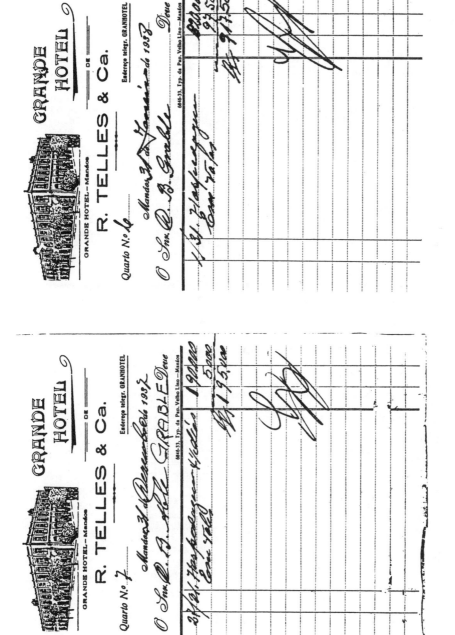

Bills from Grande Hotel, owned by Ramon Telles.

D.B.Grable expense acct.Dec.I.to Dec.3I.

```
                                                                      $
Iquitos Dec.I to Dec.2I,Hotel Meals,Laundry,and Misc.------ 70.00
Food stuffs for trip to Manaos-------- ---------------- 15.00
Hammock sheetblanket towels ect.-------------- --------   7.50
Brazilian visa---------------------------- --- --------------- 5.00
Peruvian police papers pictures & stamps.-------------------  4.00
Passage from Iquitos to Manacapuru ------- ------------- 20.00
Fleteros handling baggage------------ -- --------- -------   2.50
Stamps Iquitos------------------------------------------ IO.00
Tips houseboy------------------ --- ---------- ----------   5.00
Dec.22 to Dec.27.aboard Ari_s miscellaneous----------------- IO.00
Rent on launch from Manacapuru to mouth of Rio Negro-------- 20.00
Car rental from mouth of Rio Negro to Manaos---------------- IO.00
Radiograms and Telegrams ------------------------------- 42.50
Stamps.Manaos---------------------------------------------- I5.00
Hotel,Laundry and Taxi Manaos----------------------------- 22.50
Total--------------------------------------------========
Ont.the 28th. I drew 50 pounds sterling from Booth & Co.     265.00
```

D.B.Grable Expense Account Fmom Jan.I to Feb.I

```
Hotel meals & laundry--------------- ---------------------------$IIO.00
Cables & telegrams-------------------------------------------- I30.00
Launch Rent between Manaos and Bitar----------------------  85.00
Stamps------------------------------------------------------ I5.00
Thermos bottle &tarpaulin-Deck-chair----------------------- 20.00
Films and development---------------------------------------  7.50
Lunch ect.on trips ------------------------------- ---- - ------ IO.00
Car hire & taxi------ --------- -------------------------- - I5.00
Doctor----- ---------- --------------------------------------- 60.00
Perscriptions------------- ------ ----------------------------- I2.50

Total----------------------------------------------------$ 465.00
Mounth of Dec.----------------------------- --- ---- 258.00
Peruvian money on hand--------------------------------------- 75.00
Total credits-----------------------------------------------
                                                         $ 798.00
Drawn from Booth & Co.))--------------------£-50.-------- $ 500.00
Drawn from D & E ------------------------------ -------- --- 350.00
Total debits-----------------------------------------------
                                                           850.00
Total credits------ - ---------------------------------    798.00
                                                           $62.00
```

BOOTH & CO. (LONDON) LTD.—MANÁOS.

Copy of cable received from Iquitos -   Wireless -

         Sent, 28th January 1938 16.00
         Recd, 30th January 1938 12.20

     For Grable telegraph if pipes derrick tanks
Oils tractor wagon truck roadbuilder parats salved also
state probable date shipment. Bello expected Monday
awaiting arrival van.

Modelo 561 (antigo T 1)

DEPARTAMENTO DOS CORREIOS E TELEGRAPHOS
TELEGRAMMA

Preambulo	Especie	Manaos	Numero		Data 31.1.	Hora	
	Origem		Palavras		Via a seguir		Carimbo da Estação

(O preambulo é preenchido no Telegrapho, excepto VIA A SEGUIR)

Indicações de serviço taxadas		TRANSMISSÃO

Endereço

Destinatario .... m e l i t a ....
                      i q u i t o s

Hora:

Iniciaes do Operador

(Rua, Avenida, etc.)   (Bairro)

Cidade   Estado

TEXTO E ASSIGNATURA

salvaged some casing part tractor wagon truck no tanks
derrick oils roadbuilder linepipe stop arranging ship
february eight possible hundredfifty tons
                          grable

Tradução. salvo algums tubos gondagem parte tractor e caminhão
          nemhum tanque armação oelo machina construccao e tubos
          pt embarcaremos provavelmente 150 toneladas navio oito
          fevereiro.

Expedidor	Rua
Bairro	Telephone

BERRINGER & C.
MANÁOS

Cables between Agua Caliente Concession, Peru, and Don Grable in Manaus, Brazil.

3

Salvaging the

SS Miguel Bitar

Diving with the Greeks

BY LATE JANUARY 1938, we had made good progress
with our salvage operations. We had recovered the derrick,
the draw works, the boilers, drill, pipe, and casing—among
other things. However, we still needed some major machinery, such as the swivel and the Kelly which had not yet been
located. We needed to bring them to the surface for use in our
drilling operations and to meet the projected start-up date of
August first. Because of the language barrier I was unsuccessful in describing the items to the Greek divers. I had tried
translating English to German and then German to Greek—
but that didn't work. Then I tried translating Spanish to Portuguese and Portuguese to Greek—no results!

I made it known to the insurer that we were fighting a
river that was rising four to five inches a day and if we didn't
locate and recover the major machinery items soon, the drilling project would have to be scrubbed for another year, at
horrendous costs to all involved. I requested that agent Dryer

and a young German engineer, who had recently joined the insurance agency, help out on the *Miguel Bitar.* I wanted them to go with me to the wreck and to stand by while I put on a diving suit and tried to find the essential equipment.

So, Dryer and Max Lunderburg accompanied me on the next trip to the sunken vessel. While en route, I had the opportunity to cover in detail some of my concerns, especially the Greek divers who were not very cooperative and were talking about quitting every time something happened that didn't please them. They seemed to be mad at the world and spent a lot of their time bellowing at one another.

I wanted Dryer and Lunderburg to understand the liabilities involved in my putting on a diving suit and searching for the equipment. For me to do so was to the advantage of both the insurance company and my employer, but I didn't think my company's insurance would cover me if anything happened. I laid out a plan and time schedule of where I would look for the items. I wanted their word that each one of them would stand by the air pumps while I was in the water. We all agreed, and about one hour later we were at the sunken vessel.

No one can imagine how dilapidated the diving gear was. I had seen it before, but never realized just how bad it was until I started to put the suit on—there were patches on top of patches on the air hoses and on the suit itself. I began to understand why the Greeks were bellowing most of the time!

We checked our watches and my diving companion went down first. I found him after the silt and mud had cleared, and started working my way toward the location where I thought some of the needed equipment might be. After a few minutes I could see why the divers didn't like working on the third (lower) deck. There was a strong current coming through from the bow, sweeping over the deck, and it carried a great deal of silt.

We hadn't gone far when I saw the Kelly: a forty-eight-foot-long square steel bar with six-inch flats that weighed over a ton. (The Kelly goes through the rotary table and is attached to the drill string, which turns the bit.) It was laying lengthwise on the lower deck on the starboard side. There was no possible way of recovering the Kelly without taking it out through the stern. We then found, nearby, the swivel that went on top of the Kelly, and a seven-thousand-pound crate with the draw works at the very stern.

There would be no way of getting to the items without removing the panels and metal railing around the lower deck. Men with hacksaws could cut partway through the metal. Then we could use the winch lines on the crane ship to tear the rails and panels loose so the items could be pulled out from the stern of the ship. I made a mental diagram of the situation and signaled to my diving companion to surface.

Dining with the Greeks

It was afternoon when we surfaced and I was very anxious to contact the insurers to outline and discuss how to solve our salvage problems. However, the head Greek diver said no more plans, no more work—until we eat. He pointed to me and said, "You dive with us, you eat with us." I looked at Dryer and Max, and asked if they were invited too. The reply was yes.

I hesitated for a while trying to figure a way out of the eating situation without offending the men we had to rely on. No such luck. We went on board the crane ship and the mess was on the second deck. The headman insisted I sit at the head of the table while he went for a bottle of wine. After he opened the bottle, he handed it to me with a glass and indicated that I do the tasting and approving, as is the custom for most Europeans with their wine. I went through with it, to the best of my ability, okayed it, and started pouring it for the rest of the table. (I knew nothing about wine; my specialty was whiskey! Later, Dryer and Max said it was good wine.)

While we were sipping the wine, I smelled something cooking. The odor was fish and it started smelling better and better. The headman went to the galley and came out with a couple of large iron pans full of fish and then pans full of rice with pieces of black olives added to it. The fish, I am sure, was one of the many varieties of catfish that thrive in that part of the river. It was delicious. The head diver said they caught them there and cooked them alive.

After finishing the meal, I laid out a plan on how to salvage those items that were locked in place on the *Bitar*. First, we would go to the sawmill in Manaus and purchase enough 2" × 12" × 15′ boards for constructing a V-shaped deflector to fit over the bow to deflect the current out of the decks. Max was assigned the task. Second, we would obtain Brazilian help to use hacksaws to cut the metal rails and panels situated about ten feet below the surface. They could stay down one minute and rest five minutes. When cut partly through, we would tie on the winch lines and break the metal loose. Four days was the estimated time to complete the work. When we returned to Manaus, I advised Los Angeles that we had located the essential items for salvaging.

Return to Manaus: Rats

When I retired that night, long after 10:00 P.M., it was so quiet it was scary! I didn't hear one racehorse rat run from one end of the building to the other. I slept late and didn't get up until just before lunchtime. I went into the dining room and greeted Don Ramon, who had a sad face. He said the hundreds of dead rats had caused such a bad smell that one of the two doctors in town had telegraphed Belém health authorities telling them about the rotting rat carcasses. The doctor was afraid they might cause some sort of epidemic.

Belém had wired back wanting to know why there were so many dead rats. It had never happened before.

I asked Don Ramon if he knew of the Pandora's Box tale—referring to a prolific source of troubles. He said no. I tried to relate it to him and the point to be made, but he was not in any mood for it, because if any such thing as an epidemic did develop and people died, the townspeople would hold him responsible. Also, the rat trappers were saying if the situation continued, they would be out of work. They were already seeing him as a threat to their employment. And, in fact, the trappers would be looking at both of us with a jaundiced eye.

I strongly suggested to Ramon that he find out when the health officer would be arriving in Manaus and that he leave before then. We could take the launch and go to the *Bitar* site and spend a day or two there and eat some Greek-prepared fish. He said he would think about it.

Max: A Lesson About Oil Men

I went to the sawmill with Max. It was owned and operated by a young Scotsman. He had heard there was an American in town, but hadn't had time to come in and get acquainted with me. He wondered if I knew I was the only American on the Amazon at the time. He was very cooperative in cutting the boards and timbers we needed to make the bulkhead fit over the bow of the *Miguel Bitar,* to deflect the current away from the equipment we had to recover. He had them all cut and packaged on schedule.

I insisted Max hire another launch and take the timbers to the wreck. He was to be there at the crack of dawn the next day, and was to take with him, from Augusto Lima's shipyard, all the manpower required to assemble and install the bulkhead on location. Max was about my age, thirty-two, maybe a little older. He was a typical blue-eyed, blond German, fairly tall and clean-shaven. He was someone you could feel at ease with right away and he was quite intelligent. He relished the assignment and took on the project, and assured me it would be ready on time. (Note: I lost track of everybody when I left Manaus a month or so later, but have often thought about Max and how he would have made a really good oil field exploration engineer.)

When Max inquired about the reason for the urgency of getting the drilling machinery on location to meet a time schedule, my reply to him was *money.* We only had so much money to spend on having a wildcat well drilled and completed (if there was oil production) in one of the most isolated areas of the world.

Next, he asked what would happen if we couldn't salvage enough of the equipment to start up. My reply was that there were a number of different options. But, first of all, he should understand that the financing of the project was being done by a group of private investors. They had limited capital. They might elect to abandon the project and collect the insurance money. Or, they might decide to raise additional money among themselves and start up the following year. Or, they might choose to ship all the usable equipment back to the United States to the drilling contractor, pay him off, and abandon the Peruvian concession.

Max then asked if the U.S. government would help us out. My answer was no, that our government was the last place oil people would turn to for help. There was a lot about the oil industry that many foreigners and many of my fellow, oblique countrymen knew little about.

For instance, the oil industry was (and is) one of the world's greatest industries in scope and magnitude. It reaches every segment of civilization. Its development and progress had all been American. From its inception at Titusville, Pennsylvania, private American individuals had taken the industry from supplying wax for candles to supplying and developing the combustion engines driving the generating plants. The industry had developed the tools, the steels, the geologists, and the engineers to penetrate the earth's crust to great depths—never before seen by man—to locate the vast reserves of fossil fuels buried by nature.

Consequently, further progress brought a network of paved roads and highways, followed by motels and great hotels. This great network interconnected the United States. Businessmen and investors in other industrial nations had confidence in the American oil man's ingenuity to keep the supply flowing of that most versatile energy source—oil! Then and now, every bit of luxury we humans enjoy worldwide can be attributed to the American oil man.

I further told Max he was witnessing the headaches and heartaches that go with being on the front line of an oil exploration project. From where he was sitting, he was seeing some of the many risks and human sacrifices that went with such a venture. If we failed, his company and ours would suffer some heavy monetary losses. But that wouldn't be the real loss. The major failure would be not knowing if oil would be discovered in the Amazon Basin. If we did not try it now, it might not be tried for years to come. And, as I had just explained to him, the oil industry had, up to then, been an all-American show that we had shared fully with all nations. (Note: when Zane Grey wrote *The Vanishing American,* which was concerned with the hardy American frontiersmen becoming nonexistent within a few years, he could have—had he been aware—titled it *The Vanishing American Oil Man: A Special Breed.*)

The next day, Max and his launch and crew had arrived with the deflector materials three or four hours ahead of me. They had it about ready to install when I arrived. It went into place properly. We could see the divers were in a much better mood.

I had brought all the ice I could find, along with fresh fruits and a hind leg of beef to repay the divers for the good fish dinner they had given us and to thank them for their work. They were elated. I felt we had their full support, and by the following day we might be fortunate and salvage some of the items that we needed to have ready for shipment on the riverboat, the *Distrito Federal,* on February 22, 1938.

Crane ship doing salvage work on the sunken SS Miguel Bitar,
on the Amazon River near Manaus, Brazil, 1938.

DRILLING AND EXPLORATION COMPANY, INC.

621 SOUTH HOPE STREET
LOS ANGELES

J. E. BRANTLY
PRESIDENT

January 7, 1938

CONTINENTAL BLDG. : DALLAS, TEXAS
25 BROADWAY : NEW YORK CITY

Mr. D. B. Grable
c/o Booth Steamship Lines
Manaos, Brazil

Dear Don:

We have just sent you a cable asking that you remain there during the salvage operations of the Bitar cargo and to supervise the cleaning and greasing of all machinery and parts which will require this work. The Insurance company will furnish the help to do this work but it will be necessary for you to supervise it in order that we may get as complete a report as possible of the items and material which are to be re-ordered. We asked in this cable that you report to us daily the unsalvageable material. In explanation of this, we will immediately have to re-order those items of material which are brought to the surface and found to be unfit for use, or those items which are lost overboard, or in some manner declared unfit for use on this project. It may be that you can airmail us reports every few days giving us a good idea of that material which has been salvaged and which is in good condition, or which will be in good condition after you have had it cleaned. We need this information of course, but need the lost material list first so that we may start immediately having it replaced.

We would like to have a letter from you giving us some idea as to where you are staying, how you may be reached by mail and by cable. We suspect you will soon need additional funds and of course it will be quite necessary for us to know where to communicate with you other than our "long-chance guess", as at the present time.

In the course of our first correspondence you might break down and tell us if, as, and when, the barges left for the Concession and the latest "guess" as to their arrival date; also the latest "guess" on the effect of navigating the river with these later shipments of material against comparatively high water. In other words, we would like to have a good healthy report from you, including your own personal ailments.

Yours truly,

DRILLING and EXPLORATION COMPANY, INC.

By: *R W Marshall*

RWM:GS

Letter to Don Grable from R. W. Marshall at Drilexco, Los Angeles, during salvage operations on the SS Miguel Bitar.

Manaos Brazil S.A.

Jan.II,1938

Israel & Co.

Iquitos Peru.

Gentlemen:

Through the kindness of the Captain,the opportunity of sending my regards,and hoping you are well and prosperous.

You no doubt will have seen the alvarengas before you read this,and thats most of the news.

Salvage is progressing we have recoverd   pieces so far. If the river will only hold its present level for another mounth we should have most of it.

I have been telegraphing L.A.direct lately,it goes faster that way.When I first arrived here the lines were interrupted on the direct route,and I dident find that out until after I had sent your wire,so in order to save the day I sent you another wire asking you to advise L.A.

I suppose you as well as L.A. thought they had sent an imbecile down here,to be sending in such conflicting reports,but I sent the decisions of the insurance agent,no more nor no less.

Heres hoping by the time you read this a big part of our work is completed.As I have been instructed to stay here and take care of the salvage.

The trip back up the river is a prize to loak foward to,I am mrking this comparison by the trip down.

I have drawn £50 from Booth & Co.the chances are that I will need more than my letter calls for soon but will wire when I do. As soon as I have any idea when we will finish here I shall wire you to hold my mail in Iquitos.

Thanking you gentlemen for your kind cooperation;I remain ,

Sincerely yours.

D.B.Grable
Grande Hotel.Manaos.

Letter written by Don Grable to Israel & Co. during salvage operations.

Edificio Hidalgo
Plaza San Martin
Lima, Perú

January 13, 1938.

Mr. D.B. Grable
Hotel Grande,
Manaos.

Dear Mr. Grable,

You can imagine how interested I was to have
the copies of your letters of December 29th and January 6th to
Los Angeles, for they furnish the first authentic news of any
sort which we have had about the condition of and the salvage
plans for the"Bitar" and of the movement of the barges. Now
I wait word that the barges are on their way up the River and
that the salvage actually commenced as planned.

It is a relief to know that there is such a
thing as an "Arctic", small as she is, on the job and that there
are divers available, for Doug and I have been imagining that
it might be necessary to work with grappling hooks only, that
would mean that a whole lot of packages would be missed. The
pictures also give another slant, since from Israel's and other
reports, we thought the boat was bow on the rocks with the stern
completely submerged. From what you write it is going to be a
job enough as it is, but easier than we expected, providing the
river does not rise and sweep the "Bitar" off into deep water.
As to the latter, if conditions in the Montaña are reflected as
far down the river as the wreck the worst may happen because it
is raining so heavily in the Pachitea country that last week's
mail plane has been held for six days and there is no prospects
of its leaving yet, and I have only had radios from Bart and
Van for some time. Your letters are being copied and I will
be sending them out here the first of next week in the hope
that the mail road will be open by then.

Claud Kelley and Doug are still in Lima, and
Claud particularly, is getting completely fed up with the town,
and is most anxious to go to the Concession. Los Angeles has
thought he had best stay here until the barges were about due,
but I have now suggested that he be allowed to go over pretty
soon for, as you know, Lima is no place in which to be idle.

I will be most grateful if you will keep me
as closely in touch as you can with the progress at your end
for we have got to make plans of various sorts to coincide with
the arrival of the various shipments on the Pachitea.

As for the New York day game - California
and Alabama played to a crowd of 88,000 people in perfect
weather and California won 13 - 0. The first quarter was very
even with neither team able to advance the ball consistently.
Well along in the second quarter Mowbery of Alabama fumbled,

Letter to Don Grable from Drilexco agent in Lima, Peru.

California recovered and put on a 70 yard drive with Bottari
going over from five yards out on a delayed off tackle played
converted at the last moment into an end run. Chapman kicked
the ball. In the third quarter California received a kick
in the middle of the field and again went right straight to
the line in a series of power plays with Bottari again scoring
in exactly the same way. Chapman missed the goal. Alabama
had all the best of the last quarter and finally put four
first downs together and had the ball   on the three yard
line for a first down when the same Mr. Mowbery fumbled and when
practically over the goal line, California kicked out and the
excitement was over.

Bottari was distinctly the hero of the day. From
the tail-back position he must have handled the ball in nine
out of ten plays and carried it in six or seven out of ten.

The newspapers accounts have not yet come in
but we had perfect reception of the broadcast at home with
Doug, Claud and a few others listening in. Incidently on the
same day Santa Clara beat Louisiana State 6 - 0 in New Orleans.

Again thanks for the copies of the letters to
Drilexco and again please keep me as fully informed as possible
of all developments.

Yours,

Mowatt M. Mitchell

MMM:AC

Lima, Jan. 22, 1938.

Mr. D.B. Grable
Hotel Grande,
Manaos.

Dear Don,

I am grateful for the copy of yours of the 13th to Los Angeles and I am pushing copies to Van in Iquitos and to Bart at the Concession.

You are naturally fed up with the slowness of things and your close connection with the wreck, but I am taking an optimistic view and have a hunch that the salvage will go better than you think, that you will re-cover a good part of the cargo including most of the essentials and that they will get up the River in good time.

If there is anything that I can do here, don't hesitate to write or wire.

Yours,

Mowatt M. Mitchell.

MMM:AC

Letter to Don Grable from Drilexco agent in Lima, Peru.

DEPARTAMENTO DOS CORREIOS E TELEGRAPHOS
= TELEGRAMMA =

Modelo 504 (Antigo T 1)

Espécie ___ Numero ___ Data ___ Hora ___
Origem ___ Palavras ___ Via a seguir ___

(O preambulo é preenchido no Telegrapho, excepto via a seguir)

Carimbo da Estação

Indicações de serviço taxadas

TRANSMISSÃO
HORA:

Destinatario _Drilexco, L. A._ 20 Jan 7 PM

Iniciais do Operador

(Rua, Avenida, etc.) (Bairro)

Cidade ___ Estado ___

work to I twork party preparatory with part crew no dening suits slp of eegot tons expected daily salvage has been fram conm deck pipe has been cone. Last three days up to expectations River raised three fut

Expedidor ___ Rua ___
Bairro ___ Telephone ___

DEPARTAMENTO DOS CORREIOS E TELEGRAPHOS
= TELEGRAMMA =

Modelo 504 (Antigo T 1)

Espécie ___ Numero ___ Data ___ Hora ___
Origem ___ Palavras ___ Via a seguir ___

(O preambulo é preenchido no Telegrapho, excepto via a seguir)

Carimbo da Estação

Indicações de serviço taxadas

TRANSMISSÃO
HORA:

Destinatario _Drilexco Los Angeles._

Iniciais do Operador

(Rua, Avenida, etc.) (Bairro)

Cidade ___ Estado ___

Rate never raising one week color of eighty I ans to date all of eleven to the planters. Will keep each posted by nine. every Record day for ten days. floated derrick.

Sent Jan 23 at 7 P.M.

Expedidor ___ Rua ___
Bairro ___ Telephone ___

Cabled reports to Drilexco, Los Angeles, from Don Grable.

Daily report on Bitar salvage.

```
Date---------Se.No.-------Amount.------- -Boxes.-----pipe--size--total.
Jan.7      P 37         I              I          4    7.5/8   5
Jan 8       0           0              0         28    3.1/2   28
Jan 9       0           0              0       I4.7of7.5/8.7of3"I4
Jan I0      0           0              0        II.    3.1/2   II
Jan II             Moving salvage ship.
Jan I2 to I.30 p.m.                             I3      "      I3
                                                             --------
                                       -------
                                       I                      70.
```

The pipe is in good condition.The truck cab should be adjusted.

Date	Order #	Discription of Articles	Weight Lbs.	Quanity	Daily Total.
Jan.I3		II.3/4 casing 4 jts		4	70
"		3.I/2 D.P. I3 jts		I3	I7
Jan.I4		II.3/4 casing 4 jts		4	
"		3.I/2 D.P. I2 jts		I2	I6
Jan.I5		3.I/2 D.P. 29 "		29	
Jan.I6		II.3/4 casing 2 jts.		2	
"		3.I/2 D.P. 5 jts.		5	7
Jan.I7		II.3/4 casing 3 jts.		3	
"		7.5/8 " I2 jts.		I2	
"		3.I/2 D.P. 4 jts.		4	I9
Jan.I8		II.3/4 casing I jt.		I	
"		7.5/8 " I3 jts.		I3	
"		3.I/2 D.P. 4 jts.		4	I8
Jam.I9.		I¹.3/4 casing 3 jts.		3	
"		7.5/8 " 7 Jts		7	
"		3.I/2 D.P. 3 Jts		3	I0
"		2" I jt.		I	I
			I00,000 Lbs		I77 Jts

Remarks on damaged material.

to. 19ᵗʰ 12. P.m.

17 jts of 11 3/4
110 jts of 3 1/2
46 jts of 75/8.
1 jt of 2"
1 Truck Cab.

Daily report on the Bitar salvage.

VIA AEREA

```
Jan.19  1/2 day
and 20  on 20th.  II.3/4 casing 5 jts.
  "              7.5/8   "  12  "
  "              3.1/2  d.p.  4  "                            21
Jan21           II.3/4 casing 10 "
Jan21            7.5/8   "   9  "
  "              3.1/2  d.p.  7                               20
Jan22           II.3/4 casing 10
  "              3.1/2  d.p.  15                              25
Jan23.No work Saints day,and Sunday.
Jan 24  P2-7     Athey wagon sub frame
  "     Box # 1  Brands & Rotary drum     482x 4246 kilos
  "     Box # 3  Jackshaft & stopcocks    4038       "       3
Jan 25 Crate #17 sandreel & sandline      4227       "       1
  "     P10-100  II.3/4 Kerotest Valve     ?
        P37-1    Truck Chassis & motor      ?                "2
Jan.26 P37-3     Truck bed
  "     P17-1/50  16 bottles oxygen                          17
  "     P10-132&133  2 close nipples.
Jan 27 hung up in the hold.



42 jts.of II.3/4 casing
61  "   "   7.5/8   "        ALL O.K
129  "  "   3.1/2  D.P.
Truck chassis is bent beyond use,wireing and all electrical parts are unfit.
Sandline that is on sandreel in crate #17 is badly rusted.
```

Duas folhas deste papel e um enveloppe aéreo, pesam 5 grammas.

Daily report on the Bitar salvage.

SALVAGED MATERIAL FROM MIGUEL BITAR

BL No.	Numbers	Packages	Contents	Gross	Kilos	Value
5	PIO-I25/I65	4I jts.	II.3/4 casing		30022	3599.92
3	PI5-3/I02	68 "	7.5/8 "		28000	? 3200.00
?	P49-I56 up	I29 "	3.I/2 D.P.		45000	? 4500.00
I	P37-I-2-3	3 crates truck assembly			3595	?
I	Box # I	I box rotary drum brakebands			4246	? I000.00
I	" # 2	I " lineshaft & cathead			I383	? 750.00
I	" # 3	I " jackshaft & stopcocks			4038	976.00
I	" # 4	I " posts			I080	450.00
I	" # I7	I " sandreel & sandline			4227	? 750.00
3	P2-I	(I side track & wheel assembly			II6I	(?
3	P2-3 Athey	(I frame			885	(? 750.00
3	P2-7	(I sub frame			229	(?
3	PII-60	I box dhaintongs			I23	65.I6
3	P28-2	I box steel valves			59I	I727.67
3	PII-38/39	2 crowbars			I6	2.76
8	PI7-F-II7	17 boxes welding rod 5 out		?		?
8	PIO-IO0	I kerotest valve			I000	? 800.00
8	P9-884	I box iron bolts			200	? 25.00
?	P9-904-905-907	3 " core bbl.parts		? I300		? 500.00
?	PI7-B-I/50	25 tanks out oxygen			I000	? 500.00
4	PIO-IO3	I box steel valves		? 500		? 750.00
5	PII-5I	I " stocks & dies			5I	80.00
8	P9-887	I box iron bolts		? 200		? 25.00
9	P36-2	I " gas engine REPLACE MAGNETO			38	87.50
?	P6-6	I box tool joints			23I	? I40.00
?	P2-5	I bundle Athey wagon parts			33I	? I00.00
?	PII-63	I box wrenches			80.63	? 25.00
?	P9P8-936/94I	2 8" ells		?	88	? 75.00
?	P9P8-942/946	2 8" tees		?	88	? 75.00
I	Box # 28	I pipe straightner			62I	? 324.00
?	P38-3/4/7	3 boxes welding rod		?		?
?	P56-2	I drag scraper			48	29.3I
?	P9-IO0	(667 cartons fire brick) 635 brick are out not cartons		?		?
4	P9-887/890	(4 rolls rope) 2ROLLS OUT REPLACE				?
5	PII-6	I box files O.K.			82	43.64
3	PII-6I	I box chaintongs			II7	95.40
3	P22-I	I box steel chains			260	206.00
3	P49-A-I	I box tool joints			279	291.50
4	P8-IO	I cask steel chain			274	80.2I
4	P8-II	I " " "			243	62.62
4	PII-IO	I box steel forge			I80	40.64
5	P8-62	I box pistons & rubbers			25	83.64
5	P9-87I	I bundle wheelbarrow trays (2 trays Out)			8I	I7.00
5	P9-I200	I box pistons			I53	240.72
5	P9-I20I	I box rubbers for pistons			208	489.40
5	P9-I2I3/I2I4	2 boxes rock bits BOTH OUT			476	II94.60
	PII-57/58	2 bundles shovels BOTH OUT (I2-in-one-6-in-the-other			96	I8.I5
	P9-872	I crate iron pales			I2	33.[7]
	P9-A-872	I crate iron pales			I2	3.37

Salvaged Material from Miguel Bitar

B/L NO.	Numbers	Packages	Contents	Gross Kilos	Value
5	PIO I25/I65	4I pieces	II.3/4 casing	30022	$ 3599.92
3	PI5 3/IO2	6●6I "	7.5/8 " ?	28000	? 3200.00
?	P49 I56 up	I29 "	3.I/2 D.P.	45000	? 4500/00
I	P37 I-2-3	3	Truck	3595	?
I	Box # I	I	Rotary Drum	4038	? I000.00
2	Box # 2	I	Lineshaft cat.h.	I383	? 750.00
I	Box # 3	I	Jackshaft ect.	4246	976.00
I	Box# 4	I	Posts	I080	450/00
I	Crate I7	I	Sandreel & Line	4227	? 750.00
3	P2-I	I	(Oneside Wheel	I56I	?)
3	P2-3	I Athey	(Frame	885	?) 750.00
3	P2-7	I	(Sub frame	229	?)
3	PII-60	I	Box Chaintongs	I23	65.I6
3	P28-2	I	Box steel valves	59I	I727.67
8	PII-38/39	2	Crowbars	I6	2.76
8	PI7-F-I/I7	I7 Boxes	Welding rod.4 out		
4	PIO-IOO	I "	Kerotest Valve	IOOO	? 800.00
8	P9-884	I "	Iron bolts	200	? 25.00
?	P9-904/905/907	3 "	Core BBL.Parts	I300	? 500.00
?	PI7-B-I/50	25 Tanks out)	Oxygen	IOOO	500.00

4

Manaus: More Rats and Diamonds

Diamonds

RETURNING TO THE HOTEL late in the evening, I found Don Ramon had left a note in my room, asking me to call on him upon my return, even if after 10:00 P.M. I met him in his room, with his brother, Juan, whom I rarely ever acknowledged due to his surly presence. After I entered, Don Ramon said he had heard I would be leaving them on the *Distrito Federal* on the twenty-second of the month (February). Juan wanted to apologize for his bad behavior toward me because I was an American. I gladly accepted his apology and assured Juan there would be no hard feelings, shook his hand, and sat down. Juan then left the room.

Ramon continued to say that Juan's apology was not the main reason he wanted to talk with me in private. Rather, it was about the old Indian with the diamonds. The old man had heard from the town gossips about the Greek divers who could stay underwater for long periods of time. He believed great fortunes could be made if he could work with one of them when the river's level would be down—in about six months.

I asked Don Ramon why he had become so interested in the old man's diamonds—if, indeed, he even had any! He replied that he was motivated by civic duty and would go any reasonable distance to help bring commerce and industry to Manaus and the Amazon Basin. If the old man had what he claimed to have, then he, Don Ramon, wanted my help in getting the old man and a Greek diver together.

I assured him of my cooperation and agreed to work out some way to put them together without taking any divers off the *Miguel Bitar* job. I also cautioned Ramon about our not knowing for sure if what the old man had were really diamonds. If they were, he sure as hell was having a time of it trying to sell them. Also, it had been reported that Brazilian mining laws were not at all favorable to foreigners—and that included Greek divers.

I asked Ramon, again, to find out when the health official from Belém was expected. We would use that day to go to the wreck and we would carry the old Indian's message to the Greeks. If the old man could find common ground on which to deal with the Greeks, he was going to need help, and much of it, to break even.

About two days later, on the morning the health official was supposed to arrive, Don Ramon and I left for the *Bitar* on one of Lima's launches. We took plenty of ice and food and timed the trip to arrive at midday—siesta time.

I introduced Ramon to the headman. After a short time, he was able to put over the message to the Greek that he had a contact who wanted use of their diving gear and men to dive for diamonds on some kind of a partnership basis. The headman consulted the others and they said they would like to consider the offer when they finished the salvage work. They shook hands and agreed to meet at the hotel in Manaus as soon as possible.

On the way back to the hotel, I suggested to Don Ramon that he draw up an agreement whereby each party pay him five percent: five percent from the Greeks and five percent from the old Indian. The percentages were to cover the cost of handling the sale of the diamonds, payment of any taxes, disbursement of the proceeds on an equal basis, plus a little profit for himself. Continuing, I told Ramon my reason for advancing the idea of his becoming their agent: if those were genuine diamonds the old man had in his little package, and they represented six months of his diving in deep water—just think—a diver with good equipment could probably increase the production a hundredfold. And, look how the total would increase if all four Greeks were diving—four hundred times! That much production could cause the government to open a purchasing depot in Manaus, and perhaps start a boom. His ten percent could amount to much more in profits than he was receiving from the hotel.

For the next two nights I stayed up late helping Ramon draft a contract to be offered to the Greeks, through Ramon, from the old Indian man. When we finished the drafting, I suggested he take it to the only attorney in town to learn if it would be legal under Brazilian law. The attorney agreed to look it over and said he would get back to Ramon in a day or so.

Rats

While Ramon and I were at the wreckage site, the health inspector from Belém did come to Manaus and had left by the time we returned. The funny thing was, it had rained almost every day for a week prior to his arrival—and the rain had washed away most of the dead rat odor! To this day, I don't know what, if any, further action was taken regarding the smelly rat carcasses.

Preparations for Iquitos

On February 14, I went to the wreck and saw we had recovered almost all the items required for our start-up. I asked for a barge to be towed to the loading dock in Manaus so the equipment could be placed on board the *Distrito Federal* and shipped to Iquitos in Peru. I had also booked passage on the boat. The rest of the week was spent checking and re-checking the manifests with Los Angeles and supplying them with a list of other lost equipment and supplies to be replaced and shipped from New York at the earliest possible date. I tried to time all arrivals so they would coincide with camp preparations already underway at the drilling site.

The riverboat *Distrito Federal* docked on the twentieth of February in a carnival atmosphere. She had brought a supply of Carmen Miranda records, which were blasted loud and clear from every loudspeaker and amplifier in town. Port authorities had announced 10:00 P.M., February 22, as departure time and date. I took my luggage aboard early in the afternoon of the twenty-second and was pleasantly surprised at the luxury.

Diamonds and Farewell to Manaus

Later, I had dinner with Don Ramon at the hotel and was updated on the attorney's progress with the contractual agreement we had given him to look over, and which the old Indian man could present to the Greek divers. The attorney had decided it should be started from scratch, a typical American attorney tactic. I had hoped the Brazilian legal profession didn't know about the ploy. As it stood on the evening of February twenty-second, the Greek divers would load up all the damaged salvage (which was to be turned over to Dryer and the insurance company), break camp, and dock the Lamport and Holt crane ship in Manaus on the twenty-fourth of February. Then they would meet with Don Ramon and the old man.

I had left a duffel bag at the hotel for some last-minute laundry to be done. So, after dinner I picked it up and said an emotional good-bye to Don Ramon, Juan, Guilherme Johnson (my interpreter), the houseboys, and the hotel chef. Then I left on foot for the ship.

There was hardly walking room near the dock when the old Indian man appeared at my side and insisted he carry the duffel bag on board the ship. I let him take it and we went up to my stateroom. He took out the sack of diamonds and threw them under the mattress of the bed and said, "These are for you." I closed the door and reached in my pocket and took about forty or fifty dollars in Brazilian money, which I had planned to use for service tips on the trip upriver. At first he said he wouldn't take the money. But I kept insisting he do so and told him in Portuguese that he was a poor man and needed the money. He then took the money and said for me to please come back soon. He shook my hand heartily, left the cabin, and disappeared into the crowd.

The whistle sounded and the call made for "all aboard that is going aboard." It was one of the few clear nights we had had for over a week. I went to the ship's railing and watched as the gangplank was raised. In a few minutes the pulsations of the steam engines grew louder and we were away. The lights seemed extra bright as we moved out into the Rio Negro channel. For some reason I felt sad, as if I had left something or someone behind, or had forgotten to say good-bye to someone. A strange feeling for a nomad like me. Perhaps it was an esoteric sense of my never hearing of, or seeing, these people again. And, sadly, that is the way it turned out.

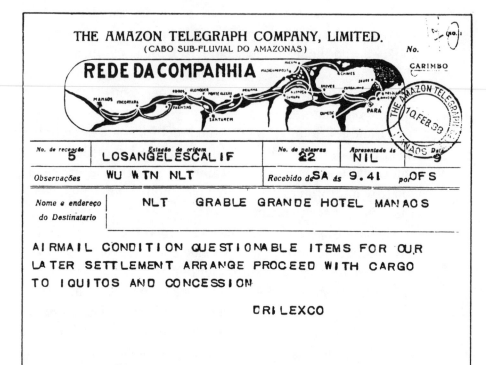

THE AMAZON TELEGRAPH COMPANY, LIMITED.
(CABO SUB-FLUVIAL DO AMAZONAS)

No.

REDE DA COMPANHIA

CARIMBO

No. de recepção	Estação de origem	No. de palavras	Apresentado às
5	LOSANGELESCALIF	22	NIL

Observações	WU WTN NLT	Recebido de SA ás 9.41 por OFS

Nome e endereço do Destinatario	NLT GRABLE GRANDE HOTEL MANAOS

AIRMAIL CONDITION QUESTIONABLE ITEMS FOR OUR
LATER SETTLEMENT ARRANGE PROCEED WITH CARGO
TO IQUITOS AND CONCESSION

DRILEXCO

Para ser attendida qualquer reclamação em respeito a est telegramma, é preciso ser acompanhada por esta forma.

Cable communications between Don Grable and Drilexco, Los Angeles.

THE AMAZON TELEGRAPH COMPANY, LIM╷╷ED.

(CABO SUB-FLUVIAL DO AMAZONAS)

4358-37

N.º ....

N.º de expedição	Expedido á	AXA	Carimbo da estação
	ás		
	por		

Estação de origem	N.º de palavras	Horas	Data	Observações

Nome e endereço do Destinatario

MELITA

IQUITOS

NO ALVRARENGA AVAILABLE.
DISTRITO SAILS, I TONIGHT. HOLDMAIL
DON
NAO POSIVLE CONSIGER ALVARENG
DISTRITO SA MIRAR ESTE NOITE

Peço que o Telegramma acima seja transmittido conforme as condições especificadas no outro lado desta forma.

Assignatura D B Gride

Endereço ....

AIR MAIL

DRILLING AND EXPLORATION COMPANY, INC.

621 SOUTH HOPE STREET
LOS ANGELES

J. E. BRANTLY
PRESIDENT

January 29, 1938

CONTINENTAL BLDG. : DALLAS, TEXAS
25 BROADWAY : NEW YORK CITY

Mr. Don Grable
Hotel Grande
Manaos, Brazil

Dear Don:

In view of your cable advice to the effect that salvage operations will probably cease within a week due to the rise of the river to the point where further work would be impracticable, we have concluded that it will be necessary for us to abandon the unsalvaged cargo to the underwriters and proceed with claims for collection for damages suffered. It will be necessary that you, at that end, together with the representative of the underwriters, to make a survey of the salvaged equipment, accepting as undamaged those pieces which have not been injured and declaring as unuseable those pieces which have been ruined beyond use. All material that is not salvaged will be lost.

Of those pieces which you have recovered to date, I assume that everything retains 100 per cent of its value to us, with the exception of the automobile truck and its cab which will unquestionably have been ruined by the water and rendered unsuitable for service for our purposes. This should be declared a 100 per cent loss and the acceptance of the items refused.

You will be empowered to accept or reject any pieces of the salvaged cargo.

We are asking P. R. Behring Company of New York, who are our forwarding agents, to give you full instructions as to the procedure to be followed. Upon receipt of these instructions or, in the meantime, assuming salvage operations to be abandoned, you may be able to make some progress through the underwriter's representative in Manaos or at the scene of the stranded ship.

The shipping numbers of the pieces salvaged by you have been received and checking them off against the list, we of course have been able to determine those items which have been saved. However, as a double check, we would request that you write us immediately each package salvaged together with its weight as marked on the box, if still legible, and the description and condition of the material inside. This is necessary in order that we may avoid error in re-ordering to replace equipment and material lost. We expect to proceed immediately we have word from you that the remaining cargo must be abandoned, to place orders for new equipment to replace that lost.

Rec Feb. 7-38

1.

Letter to Don Grable from J. E. Brantly, President of Drilexco.

Mr. Don Grable   January 29, 1938

        Under the conditions existing we consider that your efforts in keeping
us posted and assisting in keeping the job going to have been excellent.

        We had hoped that all the heavy material might have been salvaged in
order that they might have been gotten into the river landing while the
Pachitea is still high. If they cannot be however, we shall then have to
re-order and hope to get them in on low stages of the river.

        Please continue to keep us advised of everything we need to know as
closely as possible, both by cable and letter. We shall also keep you
posted as to movements here concerning equipment replacements.

        Trusting that your sojourn in Manaos and vicinity has its compensa-
tions even under existing conditions, I am

                        Yours very truly,

                        J. E. Brantly

JEB:GS

cc: P. R. Behring Company
     89 Broad Street
     New York City

Manaos Brazil S.A.
Feb 9.1938

Drilling & Exploration Co.
621 South Hope Street
Los Angeles California

Gentlemen:

I am in reciept of your letter dated Jan.29 recieved on the
31st.also your cable dated 8th.recieved the 9th.

In explanation to the reply of your cable;had custom athorities
permitted us to check the cargo in the alvarengos while they were here
in Manaos,as I tried to get hhem to,I could have awnsered your cable
accurately,as it is I can only tell you what I have here.The resumo and
the manifest are both incorrect,so the only I see to get a check on
the lost cargo is to add what there is in Iquitos to what there is here
and check them off the packing lists,as some articles do not appear on
the list of Bitar cargo or on the resumo,making it difficult to say
where the things are you asked about.The boxes 1,2,3,4 rotary drum,line-
shaft,jackshaft,and jackposts,are here,the resumo says the frame in
box 5 is on alvarenga #7,this is on Amsco packing list,21 is the traveling block on #7 the 6" drill collar was on the Bello,the table P6-II on
alvarenga # 3 box # 300 rotary hose does not appear nor # 50 or 51.kelly
crown block and swivel supposed to be on Bitar,or unsalvaged.

Van wired from Iquitos on the 1st.recieved here the 3d.that if
possible to ship this cargo in an alvarengo,realizing that there is no
barges in Iquitos of any size,and no crane on the dock to handle heavy
cargo with,and figuring also that Israel's boats and the alvarengas will
be up the river when the Distrito arrives,I have had Paes's agent and
the Amazon River Company's agent wire and rewire to make this arrange-
ment,but seem to get little action out of them,they all appear to be
passing the buck,there being several companys interested now,each one
wants to get it off of their hands as soon as possible regardless of
how much hardship it works on us at Iquitos.

Paes has a small office here,the employees are all natives,
they have tried to help,the inertness is in Para,we wired them early
yesterday morning to tell us something one way or the other so we could
plan this loading,no awnser so far,the Amazon River Co.have an eighty
ton barge here they will let them have,it will cost them extra,not
much though,I wanted to put the casing and heavy crates in her for
through shipment,with small articles in the Distrito,this is still
pending,although it is getting late in the day and loading is under
way.

Regarding the cable I sent you on the 8th.No letter arrived
from Bhering N.Y.as to the proceedure of adjustment,since we only have
five articles to claim damages on,and the agents here concede them a
total loss,the next boat being on the 8th.March,I thought it best to
let you know how the situation is so I wont lose a mounth here if there
is nothing to do.

Report to Drilexco, Los Angeles, from Don Grable.

      The sandline in crate 17 I mentioned in the cable is badly rusted, it was a used line to begin with,it is useable,but they are willing to replace,not knowing how long it is or the history of it I asked your advice,there appears to be about 6500 or 7000 ft.its 5/8 line.I dont think it would be asking too much for a replacement,to be made.

      This cargo must all go on to its destignation before it can be abandon -oned,Berringer & Co.have appointed an agent in Iquitosto handle this work,they are Straussburger & Co.

      On the last mail I sent you a list of cargo salvaged,also explain- ing how I intended to send the last part of it in,the plan missfired,I couldent get away from here until to late to get back in time to send a letter down by the pilot,so as soon as I got the numbers I had Berringer wire their office in Para to write you airmail,the rates being very reasonable between here and Para,I hope I dident confuse you with these gymnastics.

      The cargo is being double checked in loading and I am writing O.K. behind each article,this has given me a chance to look everything over again,it is all O.Kother than the five pieces marked total loss.

               Feb.16,

No word from Para regarding alvarenga and we are loading the heavy cargo,Iwill wire Van this afternoon that the whole cargo will be on the Distrito.

      By the time this letter reaches you the Distrito should be getting close to Iquitos,she should make it up there in 15 or 16 days.

      Inclosed is another copy of the list of salvaged material,these boxes have all been opened and renailed,some of the numbers were gone and I got the weights and the content and checked it with the packing list,to get the order number.on some of these orders the only part of packages were recoverd,so I put a quesyion mark in front of the weight colum the same with the value coltum,I have tried to keep the value down in places I wasent sure of,this type of a list was nessesary for the customs here.

      I am making arrangements to leave on this boat as I feel sure I will hear from you before she leaves,if I get away on her and you want to contact me,the best way will be to wire Melita Iquitos and have him relay on down the river to different places the boats stops at,I can also awuser from these outposts if the radios are working,which they are sometimes.

      I will wire you on my arrival at Iquitos,if Van hasent advised be- fore hand.

      In the meantime I remain yours respectfully;

Agua Caliente,   Peru.
Feb. 14, 1938.

Israel & Co.
Iquitos, Peru.

Dear Sirs:-

        Arrived here after two days of bad weather had to come down
several times to get out of the rain storms. Stayed over night at a
place just below Orellana.
        According to Grables wire I suppose he is coming up on the
Distrito. If this is the case should like to have him stay there in
Iquitos until the Transhipment is made. As we have talked about I suppose you are figuring on sending this cargo up as soon as it can be
transhipped there at Iquitos, and not wait for the return of the Alberto.
        Enclosed is a circular that I promised Mr. Israel I would
send to him. The size needed depends on how heavy the work is to be.
        Below is an order for some food stuffs that I would like to
have you send up via the next boat. All of these items should be American
goods as far as possible. In the case of the string beans we do not
want those Italian beans that were sent up in the past. It is possible
that Grable can help on getting this order together while he is there.
Pinasco & Co. has some of these canned goods and wish you would do all
possible to get these things.
        1 Case Mc. Grath's canned spinach
     ?. 1   "   Libby's sausage (large cans)
        1   "   canned carrots
        1   "   "   mixed vegetables
       12 1 quart-cans Flit or equivilent
     ✓ 1 case good potatoes
        1   "   string beans
        1   "   each of canned berries and apples that are available
        6 5-LB. cans each of dryed peaches, appricots, apples, and pear:
                that are available.
        1 7 Lb. tin Sultana raisons
        1 Kilo dry mushrooms
        1 case either Heinz or Libby chile sauce
        1 Small can Colemans dry mustard
        1 case canned beets if possible
        1 case Golden state butter
        1   "   canned grape fruit
        I realize that there will be some of these things will be hard to get
but please do all possible.
        Thanking you for all past favors and treatment received while in
Iquitos along with good luck to all future work.

                            Yours Very Truly
                            E. D. Van Marter

*How about the 8 pillows ordered in December
and only 4 sent. Please make this a total of 12*

**Letter to Israel & Company from Earl Van Marter, with refer-
ences to Don Grable. Shows supplies ordered by the crew at the
Agua Caliente Concession.**

5

The Journey to Iquitos: The Distrito Federal *and Pete*

On Board the Distrito Federal

WITH THE EXCEPTION OF THE WINE I had with the Greek divers' meal back at the *Miguel Bitar* salvage site, I had not had a "hard" drink since meeting with the British counsel several weeks before, when we quaffed a couple of bottles of Old Smuggler. Feeling somewhat blue upon my departure from Manaus and the friends I had made there, I went to the bar for a drink. There were three or four small tables and a bartender. I introduced myself and ordered a scotch and soda. Suddenly, I remembered the old Indian man had thrown the sack of diamonds under the bunk mattress and the cabin steward might go in to turn down the bed. I told the bartender to hold the drink and I would be back for it in a few minutes.

I found the sack, opened it up and looked carefully at the small white and off-white stones the size of a small pea. I had one piece of luggage with a lock, so I wrapped the sack in an old sock, locked it in the luggage, and went back to the bar for my drink.

I knew I wouldn't be able to sleep, so I had another drink. I observed two young military officers on board and learned from the bartender, who spoke Spanish, that they were taking a murderer back up the river to the scene of a crime he had committed. Among the passengers in first class, aside from myself, were two young Portuguese priests, a woman with a little girl, and a customs officer. There were more cabins than passengers in first class. There were about forty people in second class, accompanied by many animals, including bulls, goats, and poultry.

The bar closed after my second drink. I walked the deck for some time and then went to my cabin and lay down on the bunk. I soon learned the cane mattress on the *Distrito Federal* was no softer than any of the others I'd had previously. So, I retrieved my hammock and devised a way to hang it in the cabin, and finally fell asleep.

The next morning I was given a seat next to the captain at a dining table. He was Brazilian-born of British parents. He was in his mid-fifties. He spoke English and was very likeable. He also knew all about what I had been doing in Manaus and told me every intelligent person in the Basin hoped we would find some oil for one reason or another. In his case, so he wouldn't have to stop every few hours to load wood for fueling the riverboats.

It was a long, boring, ten-to-eleven day journey from Manaus to Iquitos, through more of the dense, tropical jungle. We had three-to-four-hour stops at least once a day for loading wood. Some of the stops were made at night so the loading would not be so unbearably hot for the workers. The best entertainment one could hope for was eating and sleeping.

In three or four days, everyone on board was acquainted. The two priests stayed very close together. The two military officers were sociable. The woman and the little girl stayed to themselves. The crew, the captain, the first mate, the engineer, the wireless operator, and the ship's doctor were all sociable people.

But the purser was another story. He appeared to be a mestizo: about one-quarter black, one-quarter Indian, and one-half white. He was surly. I spoke to him several times and he either ignored the salutation or just grunted.

The Purser and His Bird

One day I asked the captain if the purser disliked me, or if he was just always sullen. The captain then laid it all out. The captain would have liked to fire him anytime he could have made it stick. But the purser had been with the company for over twenty years. He was a union organizer and it was rumored that he was responsible for the severe beating of some nonunion workers. He would recruit for union membership aboard the ship and while on duty. The captain managed to keep the ship close to fifty percent nonunion. All his officers were nonunion. Due to the friction between the two men, the captain suspected the purser would cut his throat if given the chance.

The captain went on to say the purser was a very strange man whose temperament seemed to be influenced a great deal by his pet bird. He wondered if I had seen the bird, which looked like an oriole. The bird lived in the purser's quarters and could get out of its cage by itself, and would frequently fly up to the crossbars atop the mast and sing for an hour or so. It would then leave the ship and be gone, sometimes for most of a day, and then return before dark. It would sit on the crossbars and sing some more until darkness set in, then fly down to its cage. Sometimes it would eat after flying and sometimes it would not eat if it hadn't flown.

The captain said that on one trip upriver the previous year, the bird didn't come back to the ship, which was somewhere near the international line at Leticia. The purser was a human disaster for about ten days. He wouldn't take care of his on-board duties and wouldn't speak or talk to anyone. The captain had a reason to dismiss him and make it stick. But, no such luck. Coming back downriver, the bird appeared at daylight one morning, all muddy and with some feathers missing. The crew members thought the bird had gone through the mating process. The purser said someone had trapped it and it had escaped.

After learning about the purser and his pet bird, I found it quite interesting to pass the time by observing them both as frequently as possible without being too noticeable. By the time we docked at Iquitos, I had come to agree with the captain—that the bird's behavior had a lot to do with the purser's peculiar personality. For example, he would start pacing up and down the deck at about the time when he thought the bird should be returning from a day's outing. When the bird landed on the mast, the purser would fold his arms across his chest and just stand and stare at the bird for long periods of time. I never heard him say anything to the bird. They seemed to communicate without talking or making sounds.

One afternoon I took my camera and went to the purser and asked him if he would mind if I took a picture of his bird. By then I was speaking Portuguese fairly well and would fill in words I didn't know with Spanish. He asked why I wanted a photo of the bird. I told him I had never seen anything like the bird's behavior, which was to fly freely anywhere it wished to go and always return to its cage every night. I was amazed that the bird could very well stay with its own kind anytime, but chose not to. Also, I told him it sang such pretty songs before it left each day and upon its return to the ship.

The explanation of why I wanted a picture of his bird seemed to satisfy the purser. He agreed to the photo session and said he would let me know the best time. About an hour later he called me over and said the bird left early in the morning and came in late, and therefore, was gone during the sunshine hours. He liked to feed the bird as soon as it came in. Whenever it was cloudy or raining—as it had been every other day—the bird would stay on board. There was seldom adequate light for taking pictures.

I suggested the solution for getting a picture might be to put extra lights in his cabin. He said he could arrange that and asked if he would then be able to have one of the pictures. I replied that if I took the pictures that very day—and there were no developers in Iquitos—I would have to send them on to Lima. The routine might take several months. I decided I would take a roll of pictures for him and a roll for myself. He could develop his roll when he returned to Belém or Manaus. He agreed.

I had a roll of Brazilian-made film in my camera, which I had partly used during the last stages of the *Miguel Bitar* salvage operation. I took about eight pictures of the bird and his owner—Mario Morales, the purser. I shot another roll for Mario. To this day, I hope the roll I gave him turned out better than mine which was barely visible.

Mario told me how he had obtained the bird. He said a woodcutter had felled a tree containing a nest with four baby chicks in it. Mario was on shore at the time, and the woodcutter gave him all four chicks. Three died in a few days time, but his pet bird had survived. It was close to four years old. He had been told by the river people that this kind of bird lived about eight years.

I asked him if he would get another bird if something should happen and the bird didn't return. His answer was: absolutely not! He would never get involved again! After that statement, he clammed up and I couldn't get him to say anything more.

Pete

I was fascinated by the man and his pet bird. As far back as I could remember, I had heard stories about humans and nonhumans (animals of all sorts with circulating blood systems) communicating with one another in strange ways. In fact, I had quite an exceptional experience with a mule when I first arrived in Peru. I thought to myself, Mario and his bird would take second place to me and Pete, the mule! I decided to tell Mario Morales the story of Pete, as best I could in broken Portuguese. Here it is . . .

It was 1921 and I was staying with an American mining engineer in Huancabamba, Peru, waiting for the rains to let up long enough before starting a prospecting trip to San Ignacio, Peru. The engineer, C. R. Keller, had a rented house in the center of town. The town had about twenty-five hundred people and was located on the Huancabamba River, about six thousand feet above sea level. It was an ancient Inca city. The house had a rock-fence corral about seventy-five feet square. Both house and corral were enclosed by rock walls.

Keller had five good mules he used for riding and packing on exploration trips from his headquarters in Huancabamba. He kept the mules in the corral and, when weather permitted, one of the two houseboys would take them out for three or four hours of exercise to prevent their getting too soft. Sometimes, when I could, and the weather was good, I would take out two or three of the mules, and one of the houseboys would take the rest.

All of the mules, except one, could be used to ride or pack. *The exception was Pete.* He was larger than the other mules. He weighed over four hundred pounds more than the others and he was six to eight inches taller. He was a beautiful, arrogant, and odd animal. Because of his size some of the townspeople thought that he must have come from Argentina. (Argentina is known for its excellent mules as well as its horses!) His color was beige with brown markings.

Pete had a history of being a real "bad actor." The only way a bit and bridle could be put on him was for one person to use a twister stick while a second person inserted the bit into his mouth. A twister stick is a piece of wood a yard long and two-and-a-half inches in diameter. A half-inch hole is bored through one end of the stick through which is passed a piece of rawhide which is tied into a loop about the size of a man's fist. The loop is placed around the lower end of the upper lip of the animal and twisted until it nearly paralyzes the animal. Then a bit can be placed in the mouth and the bridle halter slipped over the ears.

Pete had hurt several people by striking them with his front hooves, and he had bucked off a few others after they had saddled him. It was for these reasons that Keller was able to purchase Pete cheaply. I—being a fresh kid out of the Tampa Bay swamp area in Florida—knew absolutely nothing about saddle or pack animals! Keller and others cautioned me constantly with safety rules applying to saddle or pack animals—whether horses or mules—and particularly around Pete!

Huancabamba has an ideal climate, and sits in a valley that is especially beautiful when the winter rains are over. We had reached the season when we were having several rain-free days at a time and therefore the trails were dry. It was a pleasure to saddle an animal and ride around the steep mountainsides. On one of those nice days, I took Pete and *mula Negra,* a classy mare mule, on a high mountain trail up the Huancabamba River. I had found a three- or four-foot piece of chain and long rope with which to lead Pete. (Pete was supposed to be chained all the time because he would chew a rope to pieces in a few seconds and would probably take off, never to be seen again.)

Trying to lead an animal with a chain is rough on both leader and follower. So, when I was away from the village houses, I dismounted and took the long chain off Pete and put it in my saddlebag. I took the other shorter chain rope and put it on him. I had violated rule number one: never take a rope or chain off Pete unless I had another one on him already!

All the way up the mountain Pete would run up behind Negra and nibble at her withers. Then he would run up ahead of her on the narrow trail and try to force us off the road. He would shake and flop his head. It dawned on me he was having a hell of a good time! He kept up the routine until we came to a wide spot on the road where it forked into different trails. There was a little stream there, so I stopped, unsaddled Negra and watered them both.

I had brought a couple of bananas to eat and sat down on a rock and peeled one of them. I threw part of one peeling to Negra. I started to throw the other half to Pete, but decided to see if he would come and get it. To my delight and surprise, he hesitated for a second, and then came up to me and took the peeling out of my hand.

The thought crossed my mind that the mule was trying to say something and that maybe he was jealous of my riding Negra—with all that business of cutting us off in the tight places on the trail, nibbling her flanks, and flopping his head. Pete's behavior was certainly something altogether different from what I had heard about him. Since he seemed to be in such a good mood, I decided to test him out.

I took the bit and bridle off Negra and very slowly walked over to Pete and put my hand on his neck. He showed no signs of hostility or resistance. I placed the bit in his mouth and raised the leather straps over his ears. I had been told if I ever touched his ears, he would rise and strike at me with his front hooves. However, he seemed to be perfectly at ease.

I hesitated for a moment about putting the saddle on him, but looked him in the eye and got the feeling I was doing what he wanted me to do. I placed the saddle blankets on his back, then the saddle, and cinched it up. Pete was not tied up to anything while I saddled him, although about twenty feet of rope was dangling around his neck all during the saddling operation. I coiled Negra's lead rope in one hand, mounted Pete, and we started down the mountain toward Huanca-bamba. On a flat area or two, I reined him in and made him single-foot. At another place I let him gallop, which he seemed to enjoy. All during this time, it never occurred to me what I was going to say to Keller, the owner of the mules, when I returned to his house.

Keller was sitting on the veranda talking to an old destitute Chinese man who used to come by for any foodstuffs we couldn't eat. When he looked up and saw me riding Pete and leading Negra, his first remark was, "What in the hell have you done to my mules?" Then he jumped up and ran to open the gate from the inside. The houseboys shouted to the kids gathered outside the gate that the *gringo* had ridden *el corco-vado*—the bucking mule.

I handed the lead rope to one of the houseboys so he could take Negra to her post. The other houseboy approached

Pete to unsaddle him. I saw Pete start to back up. I stopped the boy and told him I would unsaddle Pete, which I did, with Keller looking on all the while. I gently slipped the halter over Pete's ears and the bit out of his mouth. He had no rope on him and was standing perfectly still. I went over and picked up a rope with no chain and led Pete to his post. Then I picked up a big bunch of green alfalfa and dropped it at his feet.

Keller was a very intelligent man and was a keen student of people and animals. Since we had no electric lights, he ordered our dinner to be served extra early so I could relate my mule ride adventure to him in detail, starting from the time we left until we returned.

During the meal Keller mentioned the green corn and beef shortribs served American style. Peruvians didn't cut meat or cook green corn the way Americans did. The local butcher had let Keller cut the ribs. He said he had cut them American style for a special occasion. Keller asked me, "Do you know what day this is?" I thought for a moment and said no. Then he said, "This is February fifth. Does that mean anything to you?"

I had become so engrossed in a new and strange life recently—trying to learn a new language and new customs—that I had paid little attention to the dates. *My sixteenth birthday* would have gone by unnoticed if Keller, and Pete, in his way, had not called my attention to it. I thanked Keller for the effort he had gone to in serving the special birthday dinner for me. Before we said good night, he remarked it would be a birthday I would never forget. He was so right!

The next two weeks were very interesting as we prepared for a muleback trip from Huancabamba to San Ignacio via La Balsa (all in Peru). Part of the plan was for Keller to ride Pete instead of packing him, because Pete had decided to act like a normal saddle animal. I would saddle him, along with the other mules, every other day, rain or shine, until departure time, to keep them all in shape.

We gathered at daylight on the day of departure and Keller took Pete from his post and started to put the bit in his mouth. Pete jerked, pulled away, and backed up. Keller and two houseboys tried to hold him as he began striking out with both front hooves. He was snorting too. Keller had on his English riding boots and English breeches which had no belt loops and which he held up with just a wide belt. By the time they got Pete backed into a corner, Keller's jodhpurs were down around his boot tops, his bare ass was shining, and his face was as red as a beet! When the houseboys started laughing, I knew Keller would have shot Pete dead on the spot if he had had his gun handy.

Keller pulled up his pants, went over to the water barrel, and washed and dried the mud off his hands and face. Then he told one of the boys to go for the nose twister. I pleaded with him to just pack Pete if we had to, but not to use the nose twister anymore. But, first, I begged him to let me see if I could saddle Pete for him. He agreed and went over and sat down to cool off.

The boys and I packed the three other mules and saddled Negra. When they were all ready, I went over to Pete with the bit and bridle and slipped the bit into his mouth and the bridle leather over his ears. Then I lead him out of the corner and saddled him in about ten minutes. I lead him over to Keller who said, "I guess the only way I can ever ride the son-of-a-bitch is to have you around to saddle him for me!"

I stayed by Pete's side while Keller mounted him. I then lead the way out of the corral to the street and out on to the San Ignacio trail. I saddled Pete every day on the entire forty-day pack trip. . . .

To say the least, it took several sessions in broken Portuguese to relate the story about my arcane experience in somehow communicating with a nonhuman creature, to Mario, the purser, who did the same type of thing with his pet bird. When I said good-bye to Mario, I looked into his eyes and I could see something other than the bitterness and hatred for which he was known.

Most cases I have heard about regarding humans communicating with animals, or nonhuman beings, are very odd happenings. Many cases deal with such creatures as exotic birds, porpoises, beautiful dogs, etc. But what in the world did I have which enabled me to transmit some kind of message to Pete, that hybrid animal—the biggest and the loudest-farting pack mule in all of Peru? I don't know! But, believe me, I will never, ever forget him!

Tickets for passage on the Distrito Federal for Don Grable.

6

Arrival and Times at Agua Caliente

Iquitos

WE DOCKED AT IQUITOS, PERU, early in the morning of March 4, 1938, and cleared customs in a matter of a few minutes. Israel, the import-export businessman who had helped on my previous stay three months earlier, met me at the dock. He told me there was a great deal of mail and several cablegrams waiting for me at his office. We agreed to meet for lunch so I could go over the messages and letters.

I checked into the same room at the hotel that I had on the earlier visit—no running water or inside toilets. A while later, after leaving to meet Israel, I remembered that to go through customs with no problems, I had taken the sack of diamonds the old man had given me from the locked bag and put them in my hip pocket. Not wanting to carry them on my person, I returned to the hotel and put them in the locked bag. I had not yet counted the number of stones in the sack, as I was reluctant to open them up while on the Brazilian ship.

Cables from the Los Angeles office stated they wanted me to have business in Iquitos finalized as soon as possible. I was to get myself to Agua Caliente to relieve Bart Gillespie (a California oil man, who had come down on a short assignment to locate and build a river port), start a road up to the main camp where the well was to be drilled, and ready several things for the building of the main camp.

Before leaving for Agua Caliente, I saw to it that the recovered critical items and equipment were unloaded from the *Distrito Federal* and put on an *alvarenga* (barge) to be taken upriver to the Pachitea River and the concession port. The military sent a flying pontoon boat with a 250-pound pilot to pick up a Peruvian national and me and fly us to Pucallpa. We were at dockside at 7:00 A.M., ready to depart, but the pilot didn't show until 10:00 A.M. The river was as slick as glass with heat-waves dancing across it.

On the little aircraft, we loaded our baggage along with some extra cargo and the mail. We made a long run up the river for takeoff, but couldn't get airborne. There were too many water lilies catching on the pontoons. The pilot sent for a couple of motorized canoes, which ran in front of us and created waves to help the lift, but with no results. We had to stop and refuel after each aborted try. Soon it was noontime and getting very hot, and the water was even glassier.

We unloaded about a hundred pounds of the cargo and tied the aircraft to the pier with a rope and slipknot. It was so arranged that when the plane's motor reached its maximum revolutions, the slipknot would release the aircraft. The motorized canoes went ahead and the rope man released the rope. We were almost airborne on the first run. We docked again. The pilot was sweating like a Southern Baptist preacher and was about ready to scrub the takeoff when I suggested to him that we follow the previous procedure; but instead of losing the thirty seconds on slipping the knot, why not have the rope man use a machete and cut the rope for a faster release.

We all boarded again and followed the new plan. The rope man cut the rope with one whack of his machete and we ran just about to the end of the canoe ripples, and were in the air. We very slowly gained enough altitude to get above the treetops, and left for Pucallpa. We arrived too late to take the company canoes to Agua Caliente, so I stayed overnight at the Pucallpa Hotel—not a deluxe one.

Arrival at Agua Caliente

From Pucallpa to Agua Caliente it was a four-hour canoe ride using twenty-horsepower Johnson outboard motors. Usually two canoes made the run together just in case of mechanical problems, and especially since that part of the river was loaded with piranhas (very dangerous fish!) at certain times of the year.

I docked at the river camp about noon and was welcomed by Earl Van Marter (superintendent in charge of operations), Bart Gillespie (the engineer), Doug Fife (the resident geologist), Sam Mole (an American I had met back in 1921, when my father and I had come to Peru), Hank Hawkins (an Englishman I had also met in 1921), and Al Aish (a New Zealand missionary who had been sent to Pucallpa and who had married a Peruvian woman with whom he had several children). It was quite a motley crew of foreigners. There was Julio Mejias, the Peruvian bookkeeper who spoke English, and Roberto, the houseboy who was somewhat crippled by polio and didn't speak any English.

I brought them all up to date on how long it would be before the unloading of equipment would begin at the Agua Caliente port. Thirty days would be the earliest we could get started. We advised Los Angeles to hold the other drillers in California until we could use them.

The next few days were spent working out the logistics of installing a radio station at the port—one that would have an aerial on high ground several miles from the port. I took charge of the chore. I found the highest point on the concession to install the aerial and prepared a pathway (through the jungle from the hilltop to the radio house) along which we could lay the wire when it arrived on a supply barge.

When Bart Gillespie was preparing to leave for home, I showed him the sack of stones. He was a geologist, but said he couldn't tell if they were diamonds or not. He said he would take one to his son studying geology at the University of Southern California in Los Angeles, and have him pass it by the college's technicians. He would let me know the results. I gave him a fair-sized stone, which left me thirty-two. (I had counted them after arriving at Agua Caliente.)

Foods

Crops

The local people grew bananas, plátanos (a large cooking banana), *yucca* (a starchy root), rice, peppers of all varieties, onions, garlic, and also fruits such as papaya and pineapple. In some areas they also grew oranges, limes, and sugar cane. And of course they also grew coffee!

We put out the word to the riverboat traders that we were in the market to buy local food for our employees and the traders kept us well-supplied with everything except beef and pork. Animal fat was one of the items the local crew members seemed to like most. When I learned about their animal fat need, I placed orders for ten-pound cans of lard to be shipped with our food supplies. Julio would dole out the lard to the native camp cooks on a scheduled per-man basis.

Hunting and Fishing and *Cashibas* (Cannibals)

Time began to drag waiting for the arrival of the barge with the recovered equipment and machinery. For something to do, after Gillespie left, I took over managing the four hunters in charge of furnishing the camps with fresh meat.

Each hunter had a muzzle-loading shotgun (roughly the equivalent to a twenty-gauge if they used shells). Each would go to Julio the bookkeeper and obtain whatever amount of powder, shot, and caps he thought he could use on a day's hunt. While getting his ammunition, each hunter would report what he had brought in the day before. Sometimes if they didn't get anything, they would sleep out and return the next day to camp.

We did not recommend that they sleep out, unless for a good reason, because the only known tribe of cannibals living in the Western Hemisphere used the nearby hot saltwater springs for their annual salt supply. The springs were located along the riverbank. They were exposed only when the river was low. When I first went to the springs, the river was too high for me to see the steam from the hot water. (Incidentally, *agua caliente* means hot water.)

The next time I went to the hot springs, a month or so later, I could see the steam rising as we approached. We saw fragments of earthen pots which the *cashibas* (cannibals) used to boil the water with which to make salt—and which they also used for cooking other humans! They would stalk a lonely *cauchero* (rubber harvester), slay him with a poison arrow, cook his flesh in the saltwater, and eat him. The river people said that when you can see the steam at Agua Caliente, it is time for the *cashibas* to show up. The river people would stay away until the river rose over the steam.

The most plentiful game was the *cotomonos* (red howler monkey), which weighed about five pounds dressed and was a favorite meat for the river people. They also hunted: spider monkeys, deer, wild pigs, and *sachavaca* (tapir). As for birds, they hunted *pajahil* (a big, black-feathered, red-beaked bird), which was choice eating; the *pavo* (a small turkey-like bird similar to a pheasant), which was smaller than the *paujil* (a large turkey-like bird); the *perdice* (young partridge), good to eat, but much smaller than the *pavo,* which weighed about one-and-a-half pounds dressed.

I made a sixty-foot fishing seine (net) out of cotton twine which had corks made of balsa wood and sinkers made of lead shot. I showed the four hunters how to use it. In a few hours' time we could catch all the fish and crocodiles our camps could handle.

The fish and meat supply for thirty people was adequately taken care of for the time being. However, the number would double soon, when the drilling operations got underway.

The camp had been allocated three twelve-gauge Winchester pump shotguns with a case of #00 buckshot and three Colt 45 army pistols—all to be used for protection, if necessary. One day, I took one of the shotguns and joined the hunters when we learned that the *cotos* (short for *cotomonos*: red howler monkey) were moving down toward the river. All game and fish seemed to migrate back and forth with the rise and fall of the river's water.

On this particular occasion, the hunters could tell, by the ferocious noises the *cotos* were making, where to place me with the "big gun." It was a place the monkeys would pass over as they made their way through the high trees. The plan worked well. Within a fifteen-minute period from when they started moving over me, I had more *cotos* on the ground than we could carry back to camp. With the "big gun" and its fast reloading pump, I was able to shoot them out of the high trees. We got all the meat we could use without having to stalk the herd for hours. The experiment increased our prospects for more meat that would be needed when the additional employees arrived at camp.

There were many deer, but the hunters could rarely stalk one long enough to kill it with those little popguns they had.

Therefore, when the weather was good, we would all go out together and I would select a site at a clearing on a ridge and have the hunters spread out and work their way back toward me to stir up any available game. On several occasions we bagged more than one deer, along with many big birds, in a single drive. We would take a *sachavaca* (tapir) if it was late and nothing else was available.

The procedure the hunters usually followed was to walk until they could jump the game, then stalk it until the game was within a few feet of the gun barrel. They were all master stalkers and rarely missed. However, their production rate was very low; especially if game was spooky or had already been shot at a few times. When the hunters saw me shoot and kill animals that were running at full speed, or saw I could shoot birds on the fly, they would go to camp and talk about it for days. I never bothered to tell them I missed a lot more than they did!

One afternoon we brought in a big load of *cotos* and took them to the center road camp. it was after working hours and the men were sitting or lying down when we arrived. They all got up to inspect the kill. We took the *cotos* to a hillside over-looking a ravine where they would be dressed. There must have been fifty vultures flying above waiting for the dressing to start.

One of the hunters said, "Mr. Grable can take his gun and, from where we are standing, he can pick every one of those birds out of the sky in rapid succession." I could tell by the remarks that followed that there were many nonbelievers. The hunters pleaded with me to demonstrate to the camp crew how I could shoot flying birds. I asked the hunter doing the most boasting about my marksmanship, if they would eat the vultures which I killed. They all answered no, because vultures were not good to eat. I explained to them that I never killed any animal or bird unless it was for food. They were silent for a while. About the same time, a long-legged blue crane started circling the ravine. One of the hunters said they ate *garzas* (cranes). I picked up my gun and the next time the crane circled I shot him down. The hunters almost had him before he hit the ground. One said the bird would be used for feathers and for meat. The hunters had proven their point to the nonbelievers!

The pilots who flew the area around Agua Caliente were constantly looking for any signs of huts or cultivation where the *cashibas,* (cannibals) might be living. There had been no reports of life of any kind where they were supposed to be living. However, one hunter had found a deep canyon on top of a mountain from where it seemed he always brought back some game birds—the *paujils.* One day he reported finding strange footprints in the canyon. The following day all four hunters went to the place to inspect the footprints. They agreed— none of these were their own prints! I gave orders not to hunt in the area for a while.

In the meantime, a barge arrived with a one-and-a-half-ton Ford truck and a plentiful supply of gasoline, oils, and greases. The radio equipment was also delivered. My time was spent getting the radio in operation and the road up to the main camp finished so that other smaller camps could be built. Aish, the New Zealander, was a good carpenter. Once we had the light plant in operation and could use electric tools, things moved rapidly. As soon as enough rooms were completed in the main camp, along with toilets and showers, and the kitchen set up, we cabled Los Angeles to start sending the rest of the crew.

New Arrivals—the "Key" American Crew

Among the new arrivals were Claud E. Kelly, tool pusher and head driller; Cecil L. Tidwell, welder and mechanic; and Robert D. (Bob) Evans, tractor and truck driver and extra driller. Those three men, along with H. E. (Swede) Johnson, a driller and mechanic who came in a little later, and myself, made up what I call the "key" American crew for the actual drilling of the wildcat well at Agua Caliente.

Kelly, Tidwell, and Evans had flown from Los Angeles to Mexico City where they stayed overnight and "celebrated." Then they flew to Lima and "celebrated." They then went over the La Oroya Pass to San Ramon and were too sick to "celebrate"! And, when they went from San Ramon to Pucallpa, they were too sick to "celebrate" anywhere—anymore! By the time the fellows docked at the river camp at Agua Caliente, unloaded their gear, and went through the "meeting everybody routine," they were bushed—totally wiped out!

I loaded all three men and their bags on the Ford truck and started up the road to the main camp. On the way, I stopped at road builder's Camp #1. The hunters were there and they had enjoyed a good day. They brought in eight *cotos* and were in the process of singeing the hair off their bodies before cutting them up to cook. The smell of burning monkey hair and flesh was suffocating. All three of the new arrivals got out of the truck, looked around, and walked up the road to get away from the smell. They reboarded the truck and no one said a word. We unloaded their bags and I showed each one his room.

I had plenty of ice and broke out some Peruvian ginger ale and a bottle of bourbon. I knew all these hard-working, hard-drinking men and could see they were really low at the time. Evans said he'd pass—he just wanted to get in bed. Kelly said he'd have the ice and ginger ale, so I knew he was really low. Tidwell said he'd have one with me if I promised to do him a favor, which was for me to get on the radio the next day and tell the Los Angeles office to obtain transportation back to Los Angeles for him.

DONOVAN B. GRABLE

After a couple of good slugs of Old Crow, Tidwell showed some signs of life. I learned that there had been two days of partying before leaving Los Angeles, and two days of partying in Mexico City and Lima. Then they went up over the high La Oroya Pass (about sixteen thousand feet) without any *soroche* pills, and down to San Ramon and on to Pucallpa. All during their travels they didn't get any sleep, and the muggy heat didn't help. The sum total just about put three good working and drinking men out of commission.

The next morning Evans and Kelly didn't answer the breakfast call. Tidwell took some fruit juice and went back to bed. They surfaced about noon when it was very hot. I didn't say anything to Tidwell about the request he had made the night before concerning passage back to Los Angeles. Kelly wanted to find the shower. Evans just wanted ice water for the rest of the day. I had three sick men on my hands who could not make Roberto, our houseboy, understand what they wanted or needed.

It was two days later when I found out Evans and Kelly had "lost their lunch" when they had seen and smelled the *cotos* singeing on the road to camp. They had walked up the road to get away from the odor and vomited. Evans had sworn to himself that if he ever was well again, he would beat the hell out of me for stopping at the road camp to see the *cotos* being dressed!

A riverboat arrived about the time the boys had healed a little. We all went to work unloading and transporting the drilling equipment to the location. The RD8 Caterpillar tractor and the road grader were the first equipment off and in a few days we had an all-weather road from the port to the main camp. Kelly and Tidwell installed the pump and pipelines for the water supply to be used for drilling water, camp water, and for fire protection. They also installed cesspools for camp sewage—something unheard of by the river people.

When Kelly started feeling about normal, he said he expected to use every bit of his energies to getting the job completed so he could "get the hell out of here." We all agreed to his plan. He said, "I don't know about the rest of you bastards, but I have been scared ever since we left Lima and don't feel any better now."

I asked him if he knew we had invaded the *cashiba* (cannibal) territory. He and the others said no, and that Los Angeles—if they did know about it—hadn't mentioned it. Otherwise none of them would ever have agreed to go to Peru—to fight cannibals or the damned bugs! They were all ears when I told them about the hot saltwater springs and the annual ritual of how the *cashibas* stalked, murdered, cooked, and ate some of the early-day *caucheros* around the concession.

I told them how an American crew—drilling a wildcat well in the Motilone territory of Venezuela (the Motatán del Rio en Zulia), in 1924—were protected from a nomadic tribe of blowgun and bow-and-arrow killers. The tribe killed any intruders, but they didn't eat the flesh. We had made woodcutter *tambos* (huts made from palm leaves) every one hundred feet around the camp and supplied dogs and food so no one could invade the inner compound without alerting the dogs.

At Agua Caliente, not by plan or design, but just by the natural contours of the surface features and the location of the well site, we had created a compound that gave us quite a bit of security from the *cashibas*—should we have needed it. (The Agua Caliente Anticline was about twenty miles long, running in a northwest-to-southeast direction and was about eight miles wide. It was about four hundred miles southwest of Iquitos—about dead center in the Peruvian jungle.) I personally didn't think we would need any additional security precautions. It seemed to me, bringing in people, machinery, trucks, and tractors, and lighting up with electric lights would drive any *cashibas* out of the countryside. (This later proved to be the case.)

After we had erected the derrick, we often climbed it. On a clear day we had a panoramic view at least twenty-five or thirty miles in every direction. The scene made a person realize the vastness of the great Amazon Basin—a place with thousands of square miles where civilized man had never set foot.

We let the hunters, the canoe operators, the driller's helpers, and *capatases* (foremen on the road crews) climb the derrick to take a look around and see where they were and how they got there. Also, we asked if they could see any signs of where *cashibas* might be living. No signs were evident.

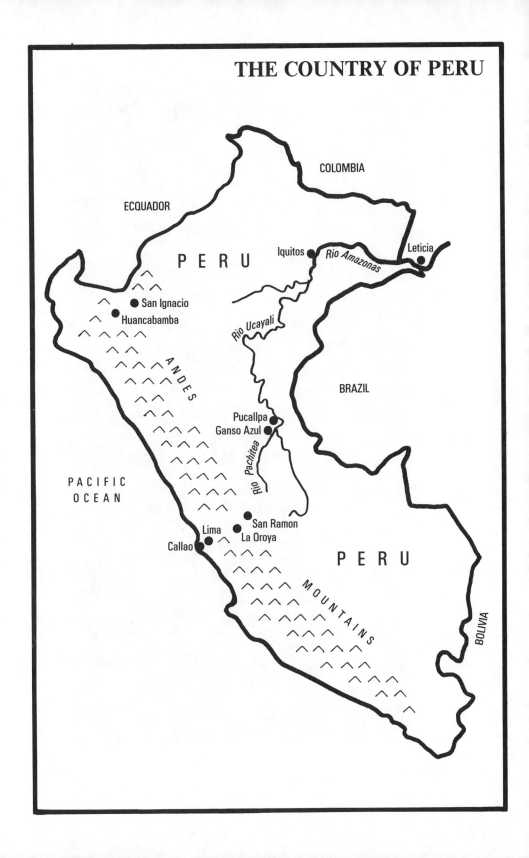

THE COUNTRY OF PERU

The riverboat Alberto bringing supplies to the Agua Caliente port on the Pachitea River, Peru, 1938.

Unloading machinery at the Agua Caliente port, on the Pachitea River, Peru, 1938.

*Don Grable and H. E. (Swede) Johnson recutting path for
placement of aerial wire for radio house at Agua Caliente, Peru,
1938.*

Radio house at Agua Caliente port on Pachitea River, Peru, 1938.

*Some of the native crewmen with a venomous bushmaster snake,
Agua Caliente, Peru, 1938.*

Tiger catfish caught by crew at Agua Caliente, Peru, 1938.

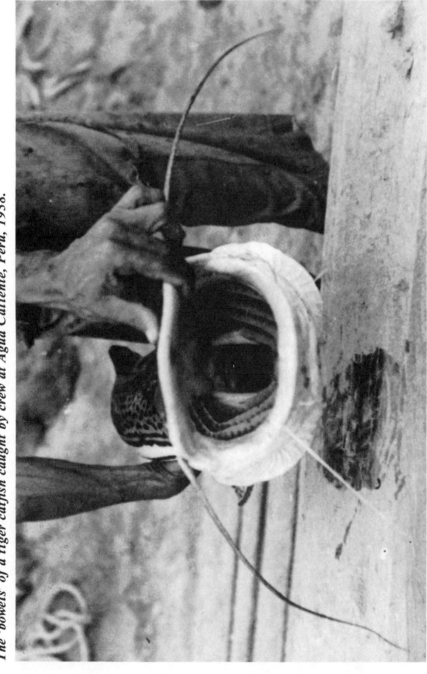

The 'bowels' of a tiger catfish caught by crew at Agua Caliente, Peru, 1938.

Several tiger catfish caught with the help of Don Grable's homemade fishing net, Agua Caliente, Peru, 1938.

Stingray caught after 'some pull' by Claud E. Kelly, Don Grable, Cecil Tidwell, and Roberto, the houseboy, Agua Caliente, Peru, 1938.

Roberto, Don Grable, Cecil Tidwell, and Claud Kelly with some baby crocodiles and mud catfish caught with the help of DBG's homemade fish net, Agua Caliente, Peru, 1938.

7

More Times at Agua Caliente

Gold and Diamonds

AS MENTIONED IN CHAPTER ONE, there had been a gold strike of considerable importance made by a Japanese miner upriver from Iquitos. The result was an upsurge in the number of trading boats traveling along all the rivers of the Amazon Basin, including the Pachitea River near Agua Caliente. Every few days they would stop at our landing before continuing upstream. About the only thing they sold the Americans was whiskey and gin. Hank Hawkins left us and went upriver to the gold strike area. We never heard from him again!

An occasional gold panner would stop and try to sell gold. I started buying when the price was right. I would pay about twelve dollars an ounce for .90 fine gold, worth about thirty dollars an ounce at a U.S. mint. Over a period of a few months, I had accumulated about twenty ounces. I knew I wasn't violating any Peruvian laws, but I wasn't too sure about U.S. laws concerning importation of gold. (At this time

Americans still could not own gold coins or bullion. However, small amounts of placer gold, such as I had accumulated, were exempt from the government's regulations.)

In mid-June of 1938, the president of Drilexco came to Agua Caliente for the spudding of A.C. #1. (Spudding is a term meaning the start of drilling operations.) As usual on such occasions, there was about a thirty-day delay waiting for the barge to bring some of the supplies needed for the boilers. During the waiting period, I had the opportunity to tell Brantly and some of the others about my diamond dealings. I told them how I had been "faked out" an earlier time—during my first "diamond" purchase—and, how I obtained the sack of stones from the old Indian in Manaus. Everyone took turns examining them and no one, including Brantly—who was a geologist—would say if these were or were not diamonds. Brantly suggested I contact someone at The Hague in Holland or at Tiffany's in New York. However, later Brantly said he would pay me double my money for them. I wanted to know what he would do with them. He replied that the mere fact that they came out of the Rio Negro in Brazil meant there was a good chance they were genuine diamonds. He said he would make a gift of them to the geology departments of several colleges in California.

I told him that four months earlier I had given one of the largest stones to Bart Gillespie to take to the University of Southern California and that I had not heard a word from him as to their authenticity.

Cashibas—Fun and Games

After drilling was underway, some of the river trading boats would tow five or six loads of people at a time up to our landing. These people would then walk eight miles up to the main camp and well site. Many times they would be in the way of the woodcutters and haulers who furnished the wood to fire the boilers used for the steam power which drove the drilling machinery.

Tidwell was quite an artist and improviser. He took a welder's helmet and attached two ten-inch horns to it and painted two big, red bulging eyes between the horns. He also took the leather welder's apron and painted red and white arms and legs all over and around it so it looked like two people wrestling. He would put on the helmet and apron, start up the welding machine, take an electrode in each hand, and then run down between the pipe racks raking the electrodes on the wet steel pipe. The result was electric sparks flying ten feet into the air, and Tidwell screaming, *"Cashibas! Cashibas!"*

The first time he used his *cashiba* scare tactic, twenty to twenty-five people took off down the road on a dead run and didn't come back that day! The longer he used the scare tactic, the less effective it became, and toward the end, people came just to see the act! Later on, Tidwell turned over the act to one of his helpers who took great delight in doing it. He would do it over and over until Tidwell would have to stop him. Grown men do childish things when they are under emotional pressures!

Washing Machine

The very first thing a drilling crew did when they moved on to a new location, and had the boilers set, was to make themselves a washtub for laundering their dirty clothes. The procedure was to run a steam line and a water line out away from the rig, where there was some drainage. Next, they would make a wooden, square box, twenty-four inches around and forty-eight inches high. It would have a wooden bottom and a hinged top with several one-inch overflow holes.

The steam line went in at the bottom of the box and the cold water line went in about half-way up the box. They would put clothes in the tub and adjust the cold water flow and the steam pressure by hand. The clothes would be washed in a few minutes. They would have to be careful with the steam or they would wind up with only a few threads and some buttons on the bottom of the box!

Because we didn't have much lumber to spare, Tidwell made a washer out of a fifty-five-gallon metal drum and placed it on a knoll between his welding shack and the native camp. After we all used it a few times and learned the right combinations, we taught the two native women we had previously hired to do the laundry how to use it. Every time they would go to use the washer, a crowd of spectators would gather around. Before long, the washer was being used constantly during the daylight hours to wash our clothes and those of all the locals. Unfortunately, it was using a lot of the steam needed to drive the drilling machinery, so we had to fence off the washing area and limit the use of the washer for those men working on the rig.

Bugs and Insects

There are a number of mechanical reasons drilling crews work around the clock—twenty-four hours in three shifts. The principal one is that the hole being drilled is less likely to cave in while the drill string is rotating in the hole and the drilling fluid is continuously circulating.

When the geologist made the location for Agua Caliente #1, he reported two hazardous conditions we would have to contend with: *cashibas* (the human cannibals) and *chicharamachos* (the bug cannibals). Included, in the orders placed by the contractor for the well-drilling machinery, were two five-foot steam-driven propellers to be placed on the drilling rig in such a way as to blow away the insects that would be attracted by the lights on the derrick and the rig floor. It is a good thing we didn't lose the two fans on the *Miguel Bitar.*

During the daylight hours, when the sun was out, many kinds of bugs didn't bother us. But when it was cloudy, raining, or dark, they came towards the lights in swarms. They came in every size and shape—from ones you couldn't see (no see-ums) to ones that were beetle-like and as large as a small turtle. All of them were hungry. Included in the bug group was the famous killer bug: the *chicharamacho,* which was about the size of a large grasshopper, four inches long, with bulging red eyes. It would come to the light making a sound like a soft Volkswagen horn. It had been reported that the bug killed several early *caucheros* in those times before people had learned to identify the bug's sound and to take cover!

When the *chicharamacho* landed on something, it would wrap its legs around the object and push a half-inch stinger into the victim. The stinger was attached to the thorax and could break off, leaving a poison spear point in the victim. It was claimed a human would not last more than thirty minutes after being stung.

According to the river people, the *chicharamachos* lived and bred in a certain rubber tree, the *espinga.* The *espinga* produces a very high quality of rubber and was much sought after by the *caucheros.* The tree grew on the higher ground, away from the rivers.

The Agua Caliente area was rich in *espinga* trees, as well as other valuable woods such as mahogany, rosewood, and ironwood. The *caucheros* could harvest rubber and cut saleable woods, all at the same time. They would use mahogany rafts to take the rubber to Iquitos. There was no way to verify the number of *caucheros,* and others, who, over the years, were reported to have lost their lives to either the *cashibas* or the *chicharamachos* around the Ganso Azul Concession at Agua Caliente.

Up until the time I left the concession, we saw no evidence of the *cashibas.* However, we heard and saw plenty of the *chicharamachos,* along with a large number of the *espinga* trees they lived in.

The steam lines from the boiler battery to the rig were exposed to the insect barrage. So, in the morning a sweeper with a rake, a broom, and a wheelbarrow would clean the dead bugs off the steam lines before they would start to smell. Hundreds of pounds of the bugs would be shoveled into the boilers and cremated to keep down the rotting smell.

I ran what is known as the "afternoon tour," an oil field term for the 4:00 P.M. to midnight shift. To have protection from the many tiny, biting insects, I would put on heavy cotton khaki pants and shirt. I would stuff my pants legs into slip-on leather boots and dump bug repellant inside the boots. I would put heavy rubber bands around my shirt cuffs and soak them with bug repellant. Then I would put on a slicker suit (rain suit) and ten-inch gauntlet gloves.

Since I was the driller, the movable propeller fans were placed so that I (as well as the other drillers) could stand near them for protection from the insects while operating the machinery. I stood by the fans as much as possible while working my shift. The fans moved enough air to fly a light aircraft and blew most of the insects away from us. Even so, at the end of my eight-hour shift, my eyes, ears, and neck would be as red as a beet from the *manta blanca* (no see-ums) bites. My wrists and ankles, both well-protected by the clothing, would, nevertheless, be red and itchy.

Standing in front of the fans, wearing extra-heavy clothing, I felt fairly well-protected. But it was different with the four men on the floor of the rig, because they wore just plain, light clothing. There was rarely a night when we didn't hear the *chicharamachos* coming. I would have to pull the main switch to darken the rig floor and the derrick. When one of us would hear a *chicaramacho* horn, he would shout, "*Bichos,*" (bugs) and each one would dive into his special protected spot. After the all-clear signal, I would turn the lights back on.

Swede Johnson, the morning-tour driller (midnight to 8:00 A.M.), had a slightly different routine from mine. He wouldn't use the lights at all unless he was pulling the tools in or out of the hole. The rest of the time he would use a hand light that he could adjust on and off and use for reading the instruments. Swede and I would compare notes every day on how many times our respective crews would hear the horn of the *chicharamacho.* It seemed to be about the same. Bright, moon lit nights were the worst. The *chicharamachos* didn't seem to fly in the rain, however.

Claud Kelly, the daylight driller (8:00 A.M. to 4:00 P.M.), never reported a single incident, and rarely did he have to use the fans.

I used to look over the steam lines when I was up early in the morning, before the sweeper would start to clean them. One time I collected a gallon jar full of some choice specimens of the many varieties of insects, including a couple of *chicharamachos,* which I pickled in some scarce alcohol. I sent them to the University of Southern California in Los Angeles with Earl Van Marter when he left for home, before the well was completed.

One thing about the many hundreds of species of insects found in the Amazon Basin—they were all ravenously hungry! Also, I have never been able to understand what so many of them found to feed on when we humans were not around! The dry season was supposed to be the "heavy bug" season, but I didn't notice any bug shortage during the rainy period!

Agua Caliente Well #1

Within a week from the spud date of July fourth, we had cored a good section of oil sand. It was enough in that part of the world to become a commercial oil producer. Actually, it would have been noncommercial in other areas such as the Middle East. But A.C. #1's location was in a small and growing captive market.

Our group wanted to complete the well and put it on production as the first well east of the Andes in the great Amazon Basin. However, investors in Los Angeles wanted a look at what was below. We soon found out. It was a hard limestone section, about five thousand feet thick, and it was almost impenetrable with the drill bits we had on hand. After weeks of little depth progress and wearing out several drill bits (which had to be constantly replaced with shipments from Los Angeles), we were told to abandon the hole, skid (move) the derrick twenty-four feet, drill a new uncontaminated hole, and complete well A.C. #1A as a producer. Within a few weeks from the time we received the orders, we had good, clean, high-gravity oil flowing into a sump. It was a time to celebrate!

All the local crew members and their wives and families were invited to a beer party and all the food they could eat. We cleared the warehouse floor, set a phonograph on an oil drum and played records, such as "You Take the High Road and I'll Take the Low Road" and "Cruising Down the River on a Sunday Afternoon." Up until that time we had been fairly successful at keeping alcohol away from the locals. However, the party was different; we were observing and rejoicing in a new way of life for the people of the headwaters of the Amazon Basin.

By January 1939, A.C. #1A was completed as a producing well. Everyone of us on the American crew had fulfilled our agreements with Drilexco. However, we knew the investors would request one of us to stay on until the company could analyze what they had and what they expected to do with the new oil production. We discussed it among ourselves and it was decided that Bob Evans, who was single, would be the one to stay on for a while longer—which turned out to be four or five months!

Training the Locals

By the time we finished drilling and completing the well, we five key Americans of the crew (myself, Kelly, Johnson, Tidwell, and Evans) had trained a sizeable group of river people to be truck drivers, Caterpillar tractor drivers, welders, electricians, firemen, rotary rig floor men, derrick men, pipe fitters, and warehouse men. All these skills proved to be tradable for them. I later learned from Tidwell, who went back to Peru for another company several years later, that many of our trainees had gone to the Peruvian coast and had found lucrative employment with other oil companies.

We were fortunate that, for our crews, we were able to pick and hire the cream of the crop of available local help from the entire upper Amazon River system. They rewarded us by making our job possible, and we, in turn, rewarded them by teaching them skills they could make a living with after we were gone.

Something else of note: we had a very remarkable safety record that apparently went unnoticed and unrecorded by responsible people, including the Peruvian government. At that first discovery well at Agua Caliente, not a single person was seriously hurt in that very risky and physically demanding operation. However, when Dr. Vidal, a Peruvian physician, took over the responsibility of health care at the camp, he ordered five lepers out of the woodcutters' camps. I had a separate camp set up for them, but didn't take them off the payroll. I couldn't tell just by looking at them that they were lepers. I couldn't distinguish between the *llagas* (large, open, and weeping sores) of a syphilitic, leper, or elephantiasis (a type of leprosy) victim. We had some people with all three kinds of diseases.

Preparations to Depart Agua Caliente

Claud Kelly had jokingly said to me on the morning after the "celebration party" for the bringing in of the well, "I will give you a month of my pay if you will get me out of here to Lima." I then realized how serious he had been earlier when he had talked about being scared ever since he had arrived on "that side of the mountain."

As it happened, the young Peruvian doctor—Dr. Vidal— arrived in camp the day we were skidding the derrick. He had taken over the responsibility of health care. I hadn't had much time to get acquainted with him, but made the effort after talking to Kelly the second time about his anxieties. I went to Dr. Vidal and told him Kelly might need some help when we prepared to leave camp for Lima. Kelly didn't know a word of Spanish and Vidal did not know any English.

Kelly had a tooth that needed attention. I told Vidal we could get Kelly into his office on the pretense of looking at the tooth. Then the doctor could check him over a little to learn if he was physically able to fly to San Ramon and take an auto over the high La Oroya Pass. I didn't want to deliver a corpse to his wife! The plan worked. The report was that Kelly had high blood pressure, an infected tooth, and a case of amoebic dysentery. Nothing too serious, but alcohol made them worse. The doctor said that when Kelly was ready to leave camp, he would give him a relaxant for the flights and some *soroche* pills for the high altitude pass.

I told Kelly that if he wanted me to accompany him over the mountain, he had to send Los Angeles this radiogram: "Need medical attention—request Grable accompany me to

Lima." The following day an answer came: "Grable to accompany Kelly, Johnson, and Tidwell to Lima."

Around the first of February 1939, we made arrangements for pontoon planes to fly us from Agua Caliente to Pucallpa, and biplanes to fly us from Pucallpa to San Ramon. At Pulcallpa, the military had heard about our success in finding the one thing they needed the most—*Oil!* They bent over backwards to assist us in every way possible. We received fast service for the two planes we needed to fly the four of us and our gear to San Ramon.

Meanwhile, Dr. Vidal prescribed Kelly's pills for maximum effect on the three-and-a-half-to-four-hour biplane flight to San Ramon. The pills were supposed to make him drowsy, but they didn't work very well.

San Ramon and Lima

The pilots flew in pairs, about wingtip to wingtip across the entire distance. If either pilot developed trouble, he could visually signal the problem to the other. Just as we started gaining altitude to fly over an eight thousand foot pass, the plane Kelly and I were on started throwing heavy black oil against the windshield. Every time a drop of oil hit the window, Kelly would flinch. At one point he gripped my hand with such strength that it turned blue. I looked into his eyes and could tell he was frantic. I said to him, "Claud, I know you are a Catholic and, if it will make you feel better, please say your prayers and Creed. I, too, know what that oil on the windshield might mean!"

We landed in San Ramon before dark and the captain of the local military greeted us. He had arranged a hotel room for us in the village. I asked the captain if he knew that the aircraft we had just flown had a bad oil leak. He replied yes he did and that they knew exactly how much air time they could get out of the oil before the engine would burn up in midair! He said we had a good half-hour of running time left when we landed. The other aircraft had over one hour of flight time before its engine would burn up! I didn't bother to relay the captain's report on the oil leak to Kelly.

The San Ramon hotel owner was a Peruvian married to a German woman. They had two blond and very pretty, young daughters. A person can't imagine the influence these young women had on four "fresh, out-of-the-jungle gringos." What the sight of young white women can do to raise a man's spirits after so long in the jungle . . . You had to be there to understand! Although young, they were well-trained and re-spectable ladies. How they could have been is still a mystery to me. And, how they could put up with the lack of indoor plumbing and the lack of privacy their father's hotel offered is also a mystery. At any rate, I give them full credit for ener-gizing the four of us to tackle the La Oroya mountain pass the next day.

We hired two cars to take us and our luggage to Lima. The road hadn't improved any, so we stopped and stayed overnight at La Oroya. Kelly was really sick by then and the *soroche* pills didn't do much good. A tired group, we checked into the Hotel Bolivia in Lima late the following day.

Three days later we traveled together from Lima to the Canal Zone where we stayed at the Washington Hotel. After a couple of days we returned to Los Angeles.

Native raft floating mahogany logs on the Pachitea River, near Agua Caliente, Peru, 1938.

J. E. Brantly (hatless), president of Drilexco, with native crew rigging up boilers on Agua Caliente #1 wildcat well, Peru, 1938.

H. E. (Swede) Johnson and Don Grable in front of draw-works (winching machinery on rig), on Agua Caliente #1 wildcat well, Peru, 1938.

Don Grable with Ignacio, a baby coto (red howler monkey), and Agua Caliente well #1 with office in background, Peru, 1938.

CHRISTMAS DAY
19 38

AGUA CALIENTE   PERU

MENU

COCKTAILS A LA FIFI

CRAB SALAD A LA VAN

TURKEY KELLY STUFFED A LA DON
CRANBERRY SAUCE GANSO AZUL
PAPAS SWONKA   PETITS POIS(ON) VIDAL
CORN ON THE BOB
ASPARAGUS CON MONTESQUILLA

PUDDING DE MOULD CON SAUCE A LA SLIM

MINCE PIE ALEJA
CAFE PACHITEA

MUSIC BY DRILEXCO SEXTET
NO GROUND RULES

Christmas dinner menu at Agua Caliente, Peru, with Don Grable's face at top, 1938.

8

The USA and Diamonds

Leave of Absence from Agua Caliente

FAIRLY OFTEN, WHILE AT AGUA CALIENTE, I had recurring appendicitis attacks. They became so severe that it was decided I should return to the States for proper medical attention and removal of my appendix. We would have frequent time lapses lasting several days or even weeks, waiting for supplies or repaired equipment, etc. I concluded it would be a good idea to make my own repairs during one of those unproductive periods, which turned out to be October and November 1938. (I later returned to Peru, staying until February 1939, to finish the completion work on the well and make camp preparations for a new American crew that would be arriving to drill additional wells on the concession.)

In early October 1938, I left for the United States. Before leaving camp, I gave one stone each to Kelly, Johnson, Tidwell, and Evans, which left me with twenty-eight.

Arrival in the
United States of America

My wife, Evelyn, and my sister, Clare, met me at Miami Airport. I didn't declare the accumulated gold or the diamonds. I still wasn't sure if the stones were genuine or not.

My sister was married to Louis Augustine—a dentist and a kind of obnoxious know-it-all. I didn't mention the gold to him, because I knew he would try to talk me out of it for nothing. However, I did tell him about the gems. He was certain a jeweler he knew in Tampa could tell me whether they were real and of what value. Therefore, I picked out ten of the best-looking stones for Louis to have examined by his jeweler-friend. In the meantime, I went into a Tampa hospital for the appendix surgery.

A few days after the surgery, I told Louis to get the stones back because Evelyn and I would be driving across the country to Los Angeles and we wanted to get an early start the following morning. Louis couldn't reach his jeweler-friend, but another jeweler, the store manager, left word the gems were of poor quality. He offered only one hundred dollars for all ten of them. I told my brother-in-law to get the stones back if he could, or take the hundred-dollar offer for them, and to send either the diamonds or the money to me in California. I never saw the money or the diamonds!

Since the Tampa jeweler had deprecated the diamonds, I treated the remaining ones casually. After arriving in Los Angeles, I gave several of them to members of the Drilexco office staff. One of the staff members said his wife worked for a lapidary on Spring Street who cut diamonds. A day or so later, I stopped in at the lapidary's office and spread the stones out on a cloth. The cutter took the largest one and scrutinized it for a while. He said he thought he could make a diamond of between .50 and .75 carat. For another stone he thought he could make a diamond of .35 to .55 carat. He said he would take some of the smaller stones in trade for cutting the two large gems. I asked him if they were of poor quality. He replied there was no such thing as a poor-quality diamond, just that the less valuable ones have a dark spot or a slight color. However, the stones I had were all crystal clear—colorless! I made the deal! A few days later, I had two flawless cut diamonds in my possession: a perfect 65-point diamond and a perfect 50-point diamond! Both were made into what is called the round-brilliant cut.

Diamond Values

Four categories are used for appraising and determining the value of a diamond: cut, color, clarity, and carat. The *cut* refers to the style or shape of the stone. The *color* spectrum ranges from red to blue to yellow. The highest "color" grade is white or colorless. *Clarity* refers to the degree of internal perfection. Flawless is the top grade for clarity, meaning internally clean and externally blemish-free. Rarely is a stone flawless. *Carat* refers to the weight of the stone. A carat weight is .2 grams and each carat is divided into 100 points. An example: a ¾ carat equals 75 points in weight, or 75% of one carat weight, or .15 grams.

Conclusion to the Diamonds

After learning about my two diamonds—and seeing for myself the beauty revealed by the expert cutting—I tried to contact everyone I had given stones to. I asked them to take their stones to the Los Angeles lapidary who had cut mine, as I had good reason to believe all of the diamonds I had received from the old Indian in Manaus were genuine, of good quality, and possibly of .75 carat or more each. (I had given away the larger gems and was left with only the smaller ones.) When I realized the probable value of the ten stones my brother-in-law and his accomplice jeweler-friend took me for, I was furious, but not surprised. I had heard him brag many times about not giving his patients credit for the gold he removed from their teeth.

For my wife—as a belated engagement ring—I had the .65 carat stone set in a gold ring surrounded by a sparkling cluster of smaller stones which the old Indian had given me. It was a beautiful ring which she proudly wore for over forty-seven years. That same diamond, which my wife bequeathed to our daughter, Linda, was recently reset in her wedding band which she wears proudly. The .50 carat stone was made into a pretty cocktail ring a few years ago, as a gift to Linda from me and Evelyn. She has worn it for special occasions.

Epilogue

ANYONE FOR DIAMONDS? is a factual, documented account concerning the almost insurmountable problems a handful of truly dedicated early-day American oil men encountered and overcame. They moved machinery and personnel into one of the most inaccessible and hostile environments known to man. Then they drilled and completed a producing oil well—the first well drilled east of the Andes in the great Amazon Basin at the Ganso Azul (Blue Goose) Concession on the Agua Caliente Anticline in Peru.

The private investors who had the nerve and determination to put their money into the speculative, hundred-to-one shot, were rewarded with the discovery of a very valuable commodity within an area where civilization would eventually be forced to expand. The countries comprising the vast Amazon Basin would become the greatest benefactors by having oil available, even at their most distant outposts.

Drilexco gained worldwide fame by being the first drilling contractor to develop an oil field in a foreign country. They blazed a trail for many other American contractors to follow, as well as those from other countries.

As for the five key American employees on the drilling crew, including myself, we received a great deal of very exciting experiences and memories for our efforts and were given a two-week paid vacation by the company upon our return to the States. After the vacation, we were all back to work at various jobs in the company's Wilmington, California oil field.

In addition, *Anyone for Diamonds?* is a narrative about my rather crazy and complicated experiences with the gemstone. One of the ironies is that over the years the two stones I finally ended up with have been appraised for various reasons, and jewelers have remarked about how flawless and exact they are.

Recently, a jeweler looked at the .65 carat diamond and commented on its clarity, brilliance, and perfect cut. He didn't want just anyone to handle the gem for resetting, so it was taken to a very skilled technician. Of course, the two diamonds have increased in monetary value with the passage of time. However, *their lasting value* is in the story of how I obtained them!

I guess you could say about my encounters with diamonds: There has been some bad news and there has been some good news!

THE DRILEXCO STORY
(Reprint)

The following reprint is from a 1950 issue of *Cuttings Magazine* published by the Drilling and Exploration Company, Inc. (Vol.4 No.2). The photographs for this article (except for the first one) were taken by D. B. Grable who is also mentioned several times throughout the article.

THE DRILEXCO STORY — *Part Six*

J. E. Brantly

Agua

Back in 1929 Robert B. Moran, a Los Angeles geologist, went to Peru for the purpose of studying the possibilities, or practicability, of building a railroad to connect the Pacific Coast with the tributaries of the Amazon River. He went from Lima across the great Andes Mountains by automobile and truck and thence from San Ramon by army plane. The route lay along the Pisches trail and down the Pachitea to Pucalpa on the Ucayali River. For his purposes, and as a geologist will, he was constantly viewing the land that lay before him on all sides. Suddenly his eyes focused on an elliptical shaped corona of trees that stood higher than the surrounding jungle land and was of a deeper color. Inside this corona he saw a flat area with a still different type and shade of vegetation. Outside the corona he saw another ridge of trees, concentric with the inner ridge but occurring around the north end of it only, and of still another shade. He then saw the tops of these giant jungle trees, like a close-cropped lawn, sloping from the inner ridge of trees toward the outer and from the outer ridge away from the center of the ellipse. To the practiced eye of a geologist, this could mean only one thing—a fold—an anticline. He had the pilot fly over the area in several directions in order that he might study the feature further.

On his return to Lima he organized a party of geologists from the States and sent them in to study the area on the ground, to prove the anticline geologically and to locate it geographically. This they did. He had discovered the great Agua Caliente anticline, some 20 miles in northwest-southeast length and some 8 miles in breadth. It has a closure and reversal of some 3,000 feet. He forthwith applied for, and received, an oil conces-

Caliente Anticline — Aerial View

Sinking *"Miguel Bitar"*

sion covering sufficient territory along the Rio Pachitea to include this and an adjoining smaller anticline.

After some several years, including more study and some efforts to finance the venture, Wm. C. McDuffie, of Los Angeles, and a group of friends agreed to supply sufficient funds to test the structure for oil. This was in 1937. Mr. McDuffie called me into his office in June of that year to discuss the matter of drilling one or more wells to test the Agua Caliente anticline. We agreed to undertake the job and after as thorough a study as we could make at that distance from data supplied by Mr. Moran, we submitted a proposal under which we made an estimate of the base cost of the well. In addition to this cost we were to receive a certain profit. Were the cost less than this estimated base cost, we would have received our base profit plus one-half of the difference between the actual cost and the base cost. Had the actual cost exceeded the base cost, we would have paid for one-half of such excess until the amount of our bonus had been consumed, after which the entire expense would have been for the ac-

count of the operators. Our proposal was acceptable to Mr. McDuffie. By some strong coincidence our estimates were correct to within a few thousand dollars.

Compania de Petroleo Ganso Azul, Ltda., was organized and financed to carry out the contemplated explora-

Going!

tory drilling. A contract was prepared and signed and we were on our way to undertaking the first foreign operation since leaving Venezuela six years previously.

A rig was gotten together consisting of used but practically new equipment. It was composed of one No. 7 four speed Oil Well drawworks, two 18-inch steam pumps, three 11-inch by 11-inch slide valve engines, five 100-horsepower, 250-pound working pressure boilers, 5-9/16-inch, 4½-inch and 3½-inch drill pipe and the various items of necessary accessory equipment. Likewise there was included camp equipment, foodstuffs, medicines, Caterpillar tractors and trucks, and such other items that we knew would be necessary in an isolated area at the headwaters of the Amazon River 500 miles and five days from Iquitos, the nearest town. During the drilling operation not one minute was lost on account of a shortage of equipment or supplies, and some hole was made each day, except on cement time. There were no fishing jobs except in the river.

The equipment selected to go was thoroughly cleaned, overhauled, painted and crated in the Emsco shops and shipped from Los Angeles to New York. In New York it was transferred to a Booth Line ship for Belem, Brazil, near the mouth of the Amazon River. At Belem, it was transshipped on to a Brazilian ship, the S. S. Miguel Bitar, and four 100-ton alfarengoes, or barges. In order that there might be no delay in shipping the equipment from Belem, Earl Van Marter was sent down to expedite the handling of the heavy equipment and to check it in and up the river.

At the same time Don Grable had been sent into Agua Caliente and to Iquitos to prepare for the receipt of the equipment. After Van had sent the equipment off up the river, he went around the continent to join Don in Iquitos.

The equipment left Los Angeles in September and was transshipped in New York in October. In early November the rig was loaded aboard the Miguel Bitar and the barges and start-

Gone!

Erecting derrick in jungle — Well Agua Caliente No. 1.

ed up the river on its 3,000-mile journey. On November 30, 1937, we received a message from Belem to the effect that the *Miguel Bitar* had sunk near the south shore of the Amazon River (Solemoes to Brasilians), a short distance above the mouth of the Rio Negro. It appears that the ship and its tow had put into Manaos, a short distance up the Rio Negro, to discharge cargo and had then proceeded down the Rio Negro into the Amazon and up the Amazon toward its destination, Iquitos, and finally, Agua Caliente. Before proceeding far the ship had to put into shore to take on wood fuel for its up-river journey. While approaching shore it had apparently rammed a submerged log, which penetrated the hull in the boiler room, flooded the boilers and sank the ship.

Catastrophe! This time we *really* had a fishing job — with half the rig in the hole. The *Miguel Bitar* carried 350 tons and the four barges about 100 tons each.

Unloading ramp on the Rio Pachitea — Agua Caliente

Drilling — Agua Caliente Well No. 1

A short time thereafter another boat, the *Bello Horizonte,* of the same line, passed, took the barges in tow and anchored them in a safe spot at Manaos.

We went into conference with the insurance company through our shipping agents, Behring and Company of New York. The shipping company was requested to move the barges on up the river to Iquitos and the insurance Company, the Royal Insurance Company, Ltd., of Liverpool, arranged for fishing tool,s commonly called salvage equipment, to proceed to the scene of the accident and commence salvage operations. They had to come from Rio. In that Don Grable spoke Spanish and Portuguese, we ordered him to proceed to Manaos and check the material recovered on the fishing job. It commenced in early January.

After a short time it became quite obvious that we would be unable to recover all of the 350 tons of equipment on the ship and would have to order replacement items.

Unfortunately we did not know what was on the ship and what was in the barges, so it was necessary to await the arrival of the barges in Iquitos and to await the completion of the salvage operations before we could reorder. Van Marter inventoried the equipment on the barges at Iquitos and Don Grable checked that salvaged from the *Miguel Bitar.* This latter amounted to about 125 tons, thus leaving 225 tons in the ship in the river. The rainy season up stream had arrived and the water had become too deep and swift for fishing. I had often wanted to send a small boy down a hole to tie onto the fish. On this job we sent a man in a diving suit.

Claud Kelly at the brake

Boiler Plant
Left to Right: "Swede" Johnson, Claud Kelly, Cecil Tidwell, Earl Van Marter.

About three years ago Dr. Alfonso Alvim, of the Conselho Nacional do Petroleo of Brasil was in Belem inspecting surplus war time floating equipment for purchase and use on the Bay at Bahia. In a dock warehouse he saw a B-J hook, tongs, subs and many other pieces of drilling equipment in perfect state of preservation. He inquired around and learned that the tools had been salvaged a few weeks before from the sunken *S.S. Miguel Bitar* near Manaos. The salvage operations had been carried on by a local outfit at a very low stage of the river. Dr. Alvim purchased the tools and had them shipped to Bahia. So—we are now using tools in Brazil that we had formerly owned and used in California and that had rested at the bottom of the Amazon River for some eight years. And now we are rigging up to drill a well for Conselho between Belem and Manaos within a few miles of the route of the *Miguel Bitar* on its way upstream! Within the infinity of time all things that are possible will occur.

Upon receiving material lists from Van Marter and Don Grable, we were

in a position to re-order the equipment that had not been recovered. In the meantime the insurance company paid us without question the $125,000 for which the material actually lost had been insured. They did not check the inventory nor did they even care to see the lists—they accepted our statement and paid off immediately.

In addition to Earl Van Marter, who was to be superintendent of all operations aside from the actual drilling of the well, and Don Grable, who was to be driller and camp boss, the men selected to run the job were Claud Kelly as pusher or head driller, Swede Johnson as driller, Bob Evans as driller and transportation man, and Cecil Tidwell as driller and welder. These men were sent down before we learned that the ship had been sunk. They stayed in Lima on a long vacation and rest until the barges had arrived in Iquitos and then proceeded to Agua Caliente to commence moving in and rigging up.

Prior to our arrival there, Bart Gillespie, an old Drilexco hand now in charge for American Independent in Mexico, had been sent down by Bob

Bob Evans and jungle friend(?)

Moran to build roads, camps, and to prepare for the arrival of the equipment, and Bart had gotten all of this work done before our organization arrived. He did a good job—as he always does.

The material that had been lost was re-ordered and shipped down as quickly as possible and was scheduled to arrive at the location in early June, provided the water in the Pachitea was sufficiently deep to permit the ship to pass up the river.

In late May I left Los Angeles to go to Peru and be on the ground in the field for the spudding of the well and until surface pipe was set. We knew little about the formations and had to be very careful to get the pipe in the right place.

I arrived in Lima in due course and prepared to go to the location. The first leg of the journey from Lima to Tarma was accomplished between nine o'clock in the morning and five o'clock in the afternoon with an hour's stop at Oroya for lunch. The road extends easterly from Lima and within about fifty kilometers has gone from almost

sea level to 16,000 feet above, crossing the Andes at the highest elevation of any highway in the world. As might be expected, the road was tortuous and steep. It crossed a rapid mountain stream many times and finally arrived on top of the pass above the lower limit of perpetual snow.

On the way up we had passed a bodega, or wine cellar, excavated in the rocky cliffs, that was claimed to be the highest wine cellar in the world. It doubtless is. In Oroya I saw my first Indians of the high plains. They are descendants of the Indians conquered by Pizzaro and have retained their ancient customs almost entirely. There were Indian girls and Indian women wearing voluminous bright colored dresses in six or eight layers that, in the overall picture, remind one of a hoop skirt. Their bodices had beautiful needlework in the colors of their fancy and they wore hats made of palm fiber, doubtless from the Amazon country to the east. The married women of one tribe had a "V" embroidered on the front side of the high crowns of their hats. For "victory," I presume. I rather expected to see an "E"* on the bonnets of the single girls. Across their backs many had great shawl slings in which they carried provisions, babies, fuel, pots and pans and numerous other accessories to housekeeping and camping requirements. These were ladies of the Altiplano who had come to the village to sell their wares and buy their needs. Also I aw my first llamas serving as beasts of burden. They were hauling coal on their backs from coal mines in the hills above to the smelter.

The town of Oroya, where the smelter of the great Cerro de Pasco Copper Company is located, is about 12,000 feet in elevation and quite high for those who are not accustomed to the altitude. The mines are back in the mountains and still higher, up to 14,500 feet in elevation. The Amer-

*"Esperanzo" in Spanish means "hope."

One that didn't get away

old Spain to the final battle of Cuzco, where he broke the power of the Incas and destroyed their empire. It was over these plains that Bolivar and Sucre led their ragged army to defeat the royal troops and break the power of Spain in South America.

Tarma in its outskirts is a mud hut and mud house town with houses scarcely distinguishable from the earth of which they are built. As we approached the central plaza we found a more modern town built within the last 400 years, while the mud structures are of architecture of many centuries past. The chauffeur drove me to the hotel, deposited my luggage in the door and left me there. Having been some several hours at a very high elevation I had commenced to feel just a little bit weary with approaching symptoms of sorroche. I decided that a small stimulant might be helpful, so I strolled into the bar, had one, or maybe two. For a moment I felt splendidly and rapidly climbed the stairs to my quarters. No sooner had I reached the top than a terrific pain entered my head and other parts of my body. I was able to get to the bed and crawl in beneath several thicknesses of heavy blankets.

About six in the morning I was called by the proprietor, an American mining engineer who had settled in the country after many years with the copper company, to start our journey down the hill. Dressing was a simple matter, for I had on exactly the same clothes that I had worn the previous day, shoes included. Downstairs I managed to drink a cup of tea and we started down the highway to San Ramon, a small town and army post at about 3,000 feet elevation, from which the mail plane leaves for Pucalpa and Iquitos. This road was carved out of the sides of steep mountains and hangs above the plunging Perené like a high, winding shelf. It was cut by Alpine engineers for a mule trail for handling

icans and Spanish-Peruvians go down to the coast for a few weeks at periodic intervals to fill their lungs with oxygen before returning for another six months' hitch in the Altiplano. The Indians have adapted themselves to the high elevation and have developed enormous chests with great lung capacity in order that they may take in enough oxygen. Also they have developed short legs for mountain climbing — an astounding example of adaptation to environment.

Leaving Oroya we crossed the grass covered rolling high plains, like a ripe wheat field, surrounded by snowcapped low (in relief) mountains. The plains slope gently to Tarma at some 11,000 feet above sea level, where I was to spend the night. Scattered over the plains were huts built of clay and grass the color of the land itself, where Indians lived who tended the llamas and sheep of the high country. Even as in the days of the Incas—except that there were no sheep then. It was over these plains that Pizarro led his soldiers of mail. It was later widened almost sufficiently to permit automobile traffic up and down the mountain, though not quite. But anyway, we passed it in a Model A Ford driven by the worst automobile driver with whom I have ever had the misfortune to ride. The most of the time I seemed to be on the outside and could look directly down at the Perené 1,000 feet below. As we went around curves on two or three wheels rocks and stones were flicked over the edge and we could hear them rattling and echoing down the canyon side and into the torrents below. One curve was too sharp for even a Ford to pass, so we had to back up and make a second attempt.

Eventually we reached San Ramon and I boarded an old Boeing biplane that had been discarded from the American mail service and sold to the Peruvians for this run. It was a single engine ship and there was only one emergency landing field on the flight, but we made it, with wings flapping and wires singing. Bob Evans and Tidwell had spent a couple of days at this field with engine trouble. Bob finally did the repair job.

Upon arriving at Pucalpa I boarded a Fairchild pontoon plane that had only just arrived from Iquitos and was to take me to Agua Caliente. The pilot had never been there and neither had I and we did not have a map. We knew the general direction, however, and aften a few unsuccessful attempts finally made it into the river landing at the lower camp. We had previously circled the derrick on the other plane and so they knew we were enroute.

It was about the 10th of June now and all the equipment on hand had been rigged up, but we were awaiting the arrival of the replacement items which at that time were in Iquitos and being transshipped onto the S.S. Alberto. After a few days of fishing, hunting and just resting, we were notified by radio, which we had in camp, that the Alberto was to arrive on

June 25. Van and I went down the Pachitea to its mouth in the Ucayali to await the arrival of the ship. We had not long to wait before she put in her appearance around the big bend.

The captain of the ship was a delightful Spaniard who had been on the Amazon for more than 30 years and had been on the expedition with Teddy Roosevelt when he "discovered" the river of Doubt. The old captain told me that there was not then and had not been a river of Doubt within his time, for he had gathered rubber along its banks on many, many trips in the old rubber days—the great boom days of the Amazon country. The river just had not been mapped. He invited us to pisco and bitters that he had made from jungle roots and then to lunch.

The Alberto was a splendid river ship of probably 800 tons capacity, with twin screw propellers and first cabin accommodations for about 40 passengers. The ship was clean, neat, and very inviting for a trip down the river. She was drawing nine feet of water, but we made it up the Pachitea without incident, even though the rivers were then at a relatively low stage, and this was 3,000 miles upstream from the Atlantic Ocean—about the same distance as though we had been on a river at Spokane, Washington, that had its outlet at New York.

All hands were set to work unloading the cargo and the first items moved up the hill to the location were firebrick. The boilers had been set, but they had not been bricked up and many were needed for a wood-burning fire box. With the arrival of the brick I took on that chore myself and built the first two dutch ovens in the battery. Don Grable was a very apt pupil, so he took care of the rest of them, but with the first two we were able to fire up and complete the rigging up job and mud mixing.

On July 4, 1938, we spudded the

first well that was ever drilled in the Amazon Basin.

During the rigging up period when we were waiting on material, and even after drilling commenced, some of us spent about two afternons a week fishing both for pleasure and to get food for the camp. The accepted Indian method was to place a net across the mouth of a small creek flowing into the river and throw crushed barbaso root into the water up-stream. This root has a poison which stuns and takes oxygen from the fish so that they come to the surface. The Peruvians, and the Americans, too, with much noise and shouting and plain fun, would jump into the stream and toss the fish on shore as they came up. On one afternoon we caught in excess of 1,000 pounds. This gave us sufficient fresh and dried fish to last for some little time. The game killed was pavo, a large pheasant-like bird, paujil (a beautiful large black turkey-like bird), small deer, wild pigs, and monkeys. The jungle Peruvians were particularly fond of a variety of the latter called "aluhuata," which is the red howling monkey. The bone pile near the Peruvian camp reminded me of a similar pile that I had seen in Havana composed of human bones. Monkey meat is quite satisfactory after you become accustomed to it, but I must admit that it is somewhat of an acquired taste and one who has prejudices against cannibalism is not likely to enjoy such a repast. But in the jungle one is not concerned with such things.

With hunting, fishing, and other diversions life was not too bad in Agua Caliente, and particularly when Swede Johnson was pulling Bob Evans' leg. Bob was very much interested in the jungle and all of its life and, of course, we all knew it. One afternoon an Indian came by with a ratty, moth eaten otter skin that Swede Johnson bought for about two soles, 50 cents. When Bob arrived from the day's work

we were all standing around admiring Swede's purchase, speculating on its value in the States and on the beautiful neck piece that it would make. We could see Bob's mouth watering. After a little dickering back and forth Bob finally persuaded Swede to sell him the beautiful otter skin for $22.00. I am not certain that Swede ever refunded the money. Probably not, knowing Swede. Another of our pastimes indulged in after dinner had to do with round chips of two or three different colors and a few pieces of pasteboard with various spots on them. I believe Claud Kelley was the most expert at this pastime and doubtless shared very liberally in the hard won earnings of the others. He certainly did in mine.

The well was located on top of a steel hill, La Cumbre, probably 150 feet high above the adjoining ravine, and 600 feet above the river. When we had reached the depth of about 200 feet in the well we lost circulation. At the time Van happened to be down at the port, and when he returned to the rig he told us that a branch that ordinarily ran clear water and emptied into the hole where we got water for the boilers was running mud. After a bit of investigation we found that our mud had broken out of the hole through a vault or joint plane and had escaped at the foot of the hill. With palm fiber, fresh mud and a few other odds and ends, circulation was regained and we went on by to set surface pipe. At 1,020 feet we picked up an oil sand that in No. 1A tested 2,000 barrels daily of 43 gravity oil. And this was the first oil discovered in the Amazon Basin that is now being used to supply the needs of a primitive people over the million square miles at the headwaters of the Amazon River.

We did not complete the well in this sand in the No. 1 well, but carried the hole down to 3,150 feet. At 1,450 feet we picked up a hard limestone and continued it to 3,150 feet. In this 1,700 feet of hard Permian or Jurassic limestone we used 100 bits in 100 days and made some hole every day. We ran out of bits and shipped them by plane to Lima, truck to San Ramon, plane to Pucalpa, outboard motorboat to Puerto Eduardo, man-power two kilometers across land to Campo Rosario, and thence by another outboard motorboat to Agua Caliente. The original cost of the bits was $110.00 each. The final cost at the rig was about $250.00 each, but they saved costly shutdown days.

At 3,150 feet the rig was skidded 24 feet and No. 1A was drilled. Casing was set at 1,020 feet and the hole bottomed at 1,175 feet. The well was completed in January, 1939, making about 2,000 barrels daily through full open 2-inch tubing. Gravity of the oil was about 43° Baumé and tempera-ture 175° Fahrenheit. After 1A was completed the old crew was pulled out and a new group sent in. Ray Ortega was toolpusher and Dick Reniers had the paper work, and such thankless jobs. Amongst the others were Buck Weaver and Peruvian drillers from the fields of Northwestern Peru. This crew drilled five additional wells for production and to outline the field.

Later a 500-barrel topping plant was designed and built out of old boilers and the like. It is still supplying the petroleum products used in the million square miles of country amongst the headwaters of the mighty Amazon. Edgar H. Clayton installed the plant and managed the operation for several years.

And thus is oil brought to people of the world by Drilexco!

Claud Kelly — Don Grable
"and thus is oil brought to people of the world by Drilexco!"

ACKNOWLEDGEMENTS

As mentioned in the preface, the material contained in this manuscript was set forth and presented to my daughter, Linda Grable-Curtis, who painstakingly helped arrange, compose and edit it, and typed and re-typed it many times. I wish to take this opportunity to thank her for her efforts. Also, a thank-you goes to my son-in-law, Terry Curtis, who helped me and Linda with several aspects of the book.

Some other people I wish to recognize and also thank for their various contributions in getting this book in its final form include: Carol Lastrucci for copyediting and proofreading; Dale Griffin who did an outstanding job of reproducing the photographs from old, faded and torn pictures; and Richard Chow for help with the cover design. Lastly, a special thank-you goes to Robert McCaffrey for his timely assistance at a crucial stage of producion, for his help with the editing and typography, and with so many other details too numerous to mention.

DONOVAN B. GRABLE.